OFFICIAL SQA PAST PAPERS WITH SQA ANSWERS

Standard Grade General and Credit MODERN STUDIES 1998 to 2002

First exam paper published in 1998.

Published by
Leckie & Leckie Ltd, 8 Whitehill Terrace, St. Andrews, Scotland KY16 8RN
tel: 01334 475656 fax: 01334 477392
hq@leckieandleckie.co.uk www.leckieandleckie.co.uk

Leckie & Leckie Project Management Team: Simon Appleford; David Nicoll; Bruce Ryan; Andrea Smith
Cover Design Assistance: Mike Middleton

ISBN 1-84372-062-0

A CIP Catalogue record for this book is available from the British Library.

Printed in Scotland by Inglis Allen on environmentally friendly paper. The paper is made from a mixture of sawmill waste, forest thinnings and wood from sustainable forests.

® Leckie & Leckie is a registered trademark.

Leckie & Leckie

Introduction

The best way to prepare for exams is to practise, again and again, all that you have learned over the past year. Attempt these questions and check your solutions against these *Official SQA Answers*. But give yourself a real chance and be honest! Make sure you work through each question thoroughly so that you understand how you got the right answer – *you will have to do this in the exam!*

Contents

G

2640/102

SCOTTISH CERTIFICATE OF EDUCATION 1998	WEDNESDAY, 20 MAY G/C 9.00 AM – 10.30 AM F/G 10.15 AM – 11.45 AM	MODERN STUDIES STANDARD GRADE General Level

1   Read every question carefully.

2   Answer all questions as fully as you can.

3   If you cannot do a question, go on to the next one. Try again later.

4   In question 3, answer **one** section only.

5   Write your answers in the answer book provided. Indicate clearly, in the left hand margin, the question and section of question being answered. Do not write in the right hand margin.

SCOTTISH
QUALIFICATIONS
AUTHORITY

©

SYLLABUS AREA 1—LIVING IN A DEMOCRACY

QUESTION 1

(a) Study Sources 1 and 2 below, then answer the question which follows.

SOURCE 1

Membership of selected trade unions

	1991	1996
Transport and General Workers Union (TGWU)	1 224 000	810 000
General and Municipal Boilermakers Union (GMB)	933 000	720 000
Manufacturing, Science & Finance (MSF)	653 000	450 000

SOURCE 2

Strikes in the UK workplace

Date	Number of strikes	Workers involved	Working days lost
September 1994	19	96 000	196 000
September 1995	35	134 000	245 000
September 1996	27	120 600	122 500

Source: *Labour Force Survey*, 1997

"Membership of major trade unions has remained constant while the number of strikes has continued to rise."

Newspaper Report

Using the information in Sources 1 and 2, give **two** reasons why the newspaper could be accused of **exaggeration**.

(Evaluating, **4** marks)

(b) "For a trade union to be effective, members should *participate* in the way their union is run."

Trade Union Official

Describe **two** ways in which trade union members can *participate* in the way their union is run.

(Knowledge & Understanding, **4** marks)

QUESTION 1 (CONTINUED)

(c)   Study Sources 1 and 2 below, then answer the question which follows.

SOURCE 1

Some trade unions feel that employers cannot be trusted. They believe that employers are not interested in their workforce, only in profit for the company. Trade unions must be prepared to stand firm against employers. Strike action is the most effective way of getting management to take notice of their workforce. Strike action is needed to force management to give workers decent pay and conditions.

SOURCE 2

Many employers now accept that for a company to be successful it needs a contented workforce. Some unions say they can work with employers rather than against them. They see strike action as a last resort as both sides lose during strikes. Cooperation leads to higher productivity for the company and better pay and conditions for the workers.

Sources 1 and 2 give different views about the ways in which trade unions attempt to solve problems in the workplace.

Using **your own words**, say what these differences are.

Mention at least **two** differences in your answer.

(Evaluating, **4** marks)

(d)

COUNCIL OFFICES
Ground Floor
ENQUIRIES
HOUSING

1st Floor
EDUCATION
SOCIAL WORK

COUNCIL OFFICES

COUNCIL OFFICES
3rd Floor
OTHER DEPTS

4th Floor
COUNCILLORS'
OFFICES

MEETING
ROOMS

"Councillors **represent** local people in a number of different ways."

Describe **two** ways in which councillors can **represent** the interests of local people.

(Knowledge & Understanding, **4** marks)

[Turn over

SYLLABUS AREA 2—CHANGING SOCIETY

QUESTION 2

(a)   Study Sources 1 and 2 below, then answer the question which follows.

SOURCE 1	**SOURCE 2**

THE SCOTTISH DAILY COURIER

Another large computer-manufacturing plant is to open in Scotland. American giants Bytecorp are to develop a new plant at Inglewood employing 500 people. This is good news for the area after recent job losses in traditional industries such as mining. However, it is thought that at least 200 of the jobs will go to highly-skilled newcomers to the area.

THE SCOTTISH DAILY HERALD

Printing and publishing firm Andrew Hunt and Sons announced yesterday that they will make 150 of their workforce redundant.

Liz Gordon, spokesperson for the company, said that the job losses came as a result of the introduction of new technology to their factory. "Our business will run a great deal more efficiently as a result of the changes," she said.

"New technology has destroyed jobs."

David Henderson, trade union official

Using Sources 1 and 2 above, provide **one** piece of evidence **for** and **one** piece of evidence **against** the view of David Henderson.

(Evaluating, **4** marks)

(b)   "It is important that young people are encouraged to work. That is why young people get special help to find jobs."

Government Spokesperson

Describe **two** ways in which the Government helps young people to find jobs.

(Knowledge & Understanding, **4** marks)

QUESTION 2 (CONTINUED)

(c)   Study the Source below, then answer the question which follows.

Benefits for families with children

Benefit	Who gets the benefit?	Number of families
Child Benefit	All families with children under 16	6·9 million
Family Credit	Low income families with low paid jobs	0·5 million
Income Support/ Jobseeker's Allowance	Low income families without jobs	1·0 million

Adapted from *Social Trends,* 1996–97

"The benefits system tries to help poor families bring up their children. Benefits only go to poor families when the grown-ups are unemployed. Few families with children get any help from the Government."

Janet Adam

Using the Source above, give **two** reasons why Janet Adam could be accused of **exaggeration**.

(Evaluating, **4** marks)

(d)

"Most single parents are women. Many find it more difficult to get suitable jobs compared to other workers."

Give **two** reasons why women who are single parents may find it difficult to get suitable jobs.

(Knowledge & Understanding, **4** marks)

[Turn over

SYLLABUS AREA 3—IDEOLOGIES

QUESTION 3

Answer **ONE** section only: Section (A)—The USA on pages six and seven

                        OR   Section (B)—Russia on pages eight and nine

                        OR   Section (C)—China on pages ten and eleven

(A)   THE USA

(a)

> "American citizens have many opportunities to influence their government to try to change its policies."

Describe **two** ways in which American citizens can influence the government of the USA.

*(Knowledge & Understanding, **4** marks)*

(b)   Study Sources 1 and 2 below, then answer the question which follows.

SOURCE 1

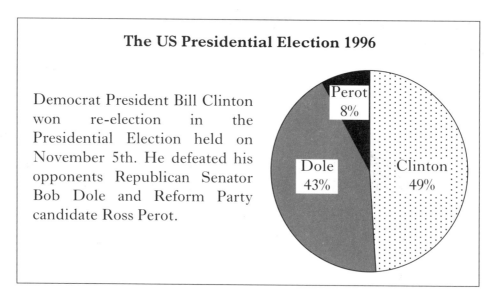

The US Presidential Election 1996

Democrat President Bill Clinton won re-election in the Presidential Election held on November 5th. He defeated his opponents Republican Senator Bob Dole and Reform Party candidate Ross Perot.

Perot 8%

Dole 43%

Clinton 49%

SOURCE 2

How Americans voted		*Clinton*	*Dole*
(the percentages of selected groups supporting the 2 main candidates)	Women	54%	38%
	Men	44%	44%
	Whites	43%	46%
	Blacks	83%	12%

Source: Adapted from *Time Magazine*, November 1996

> "Most American voters will be happy with the result of the Presidential Election."

Senator Murray K Lamb

Using Sources 1 and 2 above, give **two** reasons why Senator Murray K Lamb could be accused of **exaggeration**.

*(Evaluating, **4** marks)*

QUESTION 3(A) (CONTINUED)

(c)

> "The US Constitution guarantees American citizens many **rights**. However, along with these rights go **responsibilities**."

Choose **two rights** which American citizens have and explain the **responsibilities** which go with them.

(Knowledge & Understanding, **4** marks)

(d)   Study the Source below, then answer the question which follows.

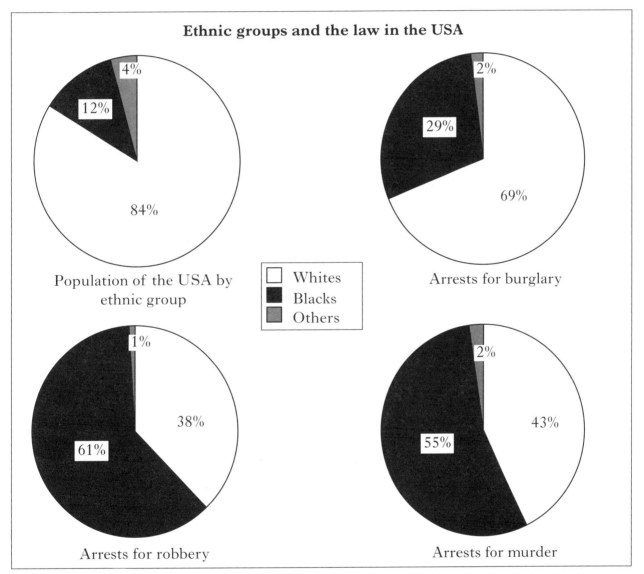

Source: Adapted from *The USA* by Clarke and Morrison, Pulse Publications

> "Many Black people in the USA believe that the system of justice is unfair to them."

Shelly Woodward

Using the Source above, give **two** reasons **supporting** the view of Shelly Woodward.

(Evaluating, **4** marks)

NOW GO TO QUESTION 4 ON PAGE TWELVE

QUESTION 3 (CONTINUED)

(B) RUSSIA

(a)

> "Russian citizens can *now protest in public against the Government.* This was not possible under Communism."

Describe **two** ways in which Russian citizens can *now protest in public against the Government.*

(Knowledge & Understanding, **4** marks)

(b) Study Sources 1 and 2 below, then answer the question which follows.

SOURCE 1

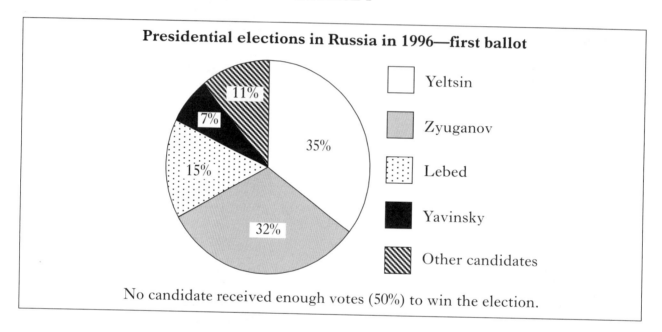

Presidential elections in Russia in 1996—first ballot

- Yeltsin
- Zyuganov
- Lebed
- Yavinsky
- Other candidates

11%
7%
35%
15%
32%

No candidate received enough votes (50%) to win the election.

SOURCE 2

Yeltsin wins on second ballot

Boris Yeltsin was re-elected as Russia's President. A second ballot was needed to decide if Yeltsin or Zyuganov should become President. Yeltsin won 54% of the votes while 40% of the voters chose the Communist candidate, Zyuganov. Opinion polls showed that only 27% of Russians trusted Yeltsin.

"Most Russian voters will be happy with the result of the Presidential election."

Alexei Kiselov, Presidential Assistant

Using Sources 1 and 2 above, give **two** reasons why Alexei Kiselov could be accused of **exaggeration**.

(Evaluating, **4** marks)

QUESTION 3(B) (CONTINUED)

(c)

> "Russian citizens now have more **rights** which allow them *to improve their living standards*."

Choose **two rights** that Russian citizens now have.

Explain the ways in which these **rights** can allow Russian citizens *to improve their living standards*.

(Knowledge & Understanding, **4** marks)

(d)   Study the Source below, then answer the question which follows.

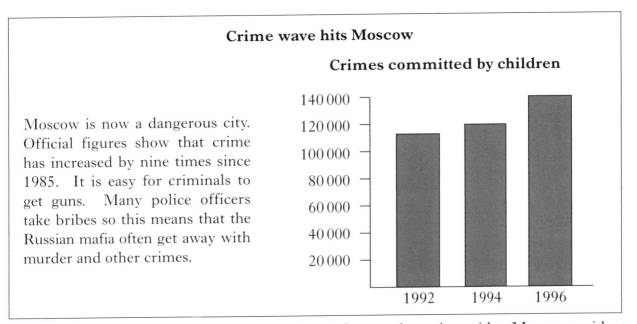

Crime wave hits Moscow

Crimes committed by children

Moscow is now a dangerous city. Official figures show that crime has increased by nine times since 1985. It is easy for criminals to get guns. Many police officers take bribes so this means that the Russian mafia often get away with murder and other crimes.

Source: Adapted from an interview with a Moscow resident

> "Crime in Moscow is out of control. Honest citizens are worried that it will get even worse in the future."

Lena Tusova

Using the Source above, give **two** reasons **supporting** the view of Lena Tusova.

(Evaluating, **4** marks)

NOW GO TO QUESTION 4 ON PAGE TWELVE

QUESTION 3 (CONTINUED)

(C) CHINA

(a)

> "In China people *cannot easily protest against the government*."

Democracy campaigner

Give **two** reasons to explain why Chinese people *cannot easily protest against the government*.

(Knowledge & Understanding, **4** marks)

(b) Study Sources 1 and 2 below, then answer the question which follows.

SOURCE 1   **SOURCE 2**

Village democracy in China

In 1987 the Chinese Parliament passed a law allowing villages their own elections for village chiefs and committees. By 1997 elections had been held in 95% of villages.

These committees make sure that no one breaks the law. They also supervise teenagers and watch over the elderly.

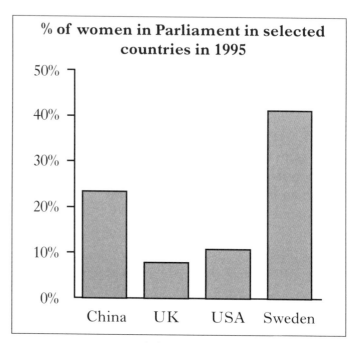

Adapted from *Newsweek*, 1995

> "There is no democracy in China. Compared to other countries, women are very poorly represented in parliament in China."

Han Suyun

Using Sources 1 and 2 above, give **two** reasons why Han Suyun could be accused of **exaggeration**.

(Evaluating, **4** marks)

QUESTION 3(C) (CONTINUED)

(c)

> "Chinese citizens now have more **rights** which allow them *to improve their living standards*."

Choose **two rights** that Chinese citizens now have.

Explain the ways in which these **rights** can allow Chinese citizens *to improve their living standards*.

(Knowledge & Understanding, **4** marks)

(d)   Study the Source below, then answer the question which follows.

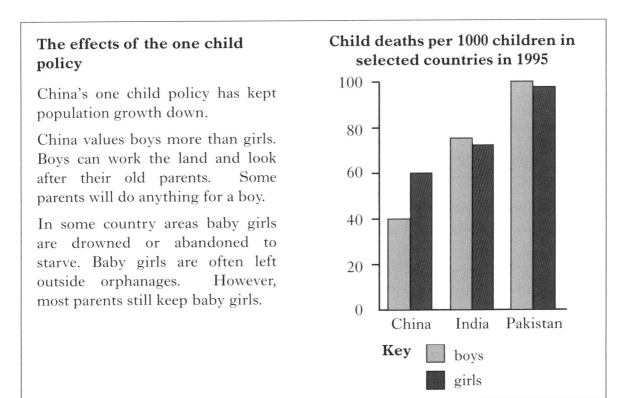

The effects of the one child policy

China's one child policy has kept population growth down.

China values boys more than girls. Boys can work the land and look after their old parents. Some parents will do anything for a boy.

In some country areas baby girls are drowned or abandoned to starve. Baby girls are often left outside orphanages. However, most parents still keep baby girls.

Child deaths per 1000 children in selected countries in 1995

Key ▨ boys ■ girls

Source: Adapted from *Newsweek*, August 1995

> "The Chinese policy limiting households to only one child causes serious problems. The death rate of young girls in China is different to other countries."

Yung Lin

Using the Source above, give **two** reasons **supporting** the view of Yung Lin.

(Evaluating, **4** marks)

NOW GO TO QUESTION 4 ON PAGE TWELVE

SYLLABUS AREA 4—INTERNATIONAL RELATIONS

QUESTION 4

(a) Study the table below, then answer the question which follows.

Country	Birth rate (per 1000 population)	Infant deaths (per 1000 live births)	Life expectancy (years)	Average annual income (dollars)
Guinea	47	149	42	450
Malawi	53	138	47	230

Source: *Third World Guide*

Using the table above, say which of the two countries should receive aid. Give **two** reasons to **support** your choice.

(Evaluating, **4** marks)

(b)

> "European countries *can benefit from providing aid to countries in Africa.*"

Describe **two** ways in which countries in Europe *can benefit from providing aid to countries in Africa.*

(Knowledge & Understanding, **4** marks)

(c) Study the newspaper report below, then answer the question which follows.

European aid pays for new airport	
Aid from the European Union has been given to build a new airport in our country.	Building the airport will provide 500 jobs for local people for three years. One hundred permanent jobs will be created once the airport is built but only for locals who can speak English.
Land which used to feed 1000 families will have to be used for the airport. This gives our country an opportunity to attract foreign tourists. They will bring in money to pay for our country's needs.	More food will have to be imported from other countries.

> *"Not all aid projects meet the needs of local people."*

Using evidence from the newspaper report above, give **two** reasons to **support** the view that *not all aid projects meet the needs of local people.*

(Evaluating, **4** marks)

(d) Choose **one** United Nations' agency and describe how it tries to meet the **needs** of countries in Africa.

(Knowledge & Understanding, **4** marks)

[END OF QUESTION PAPER]

G

2640/102

SCOTTISH
CERTIFICATE OF
EDUCATION
1999

WEDNESDAY, 19 MAY
G/C　9.00 AM – 10.30 AM
F/G　10.20 AM – 11.50 AM

MODERN STUDIES
STANDARD GRADE
General Level

1　Read every question carefully.

2　Answer all questions as fully as you can.

3　If you cannot do a question, go on to the next one.　Try again later.

4　In question 3, answer **one** section only.

5　Write your answers in the answer book provided.　Indicate clearly, in the left hand margin, the question and section of question being answered.　Do not write in the right hand margin.

SCOTTISH
QUALIFICATIONS
AUTHORITY

SYLLABUS AREA 1—LIVING IN A DEMOCRACY

QUESTION 1

(a)

> "MPs can represent the interests of their constituents in a number of ways."

Describe in detail **two** ways in which MPs can **represent** the interests of their constituents.

(Knowledge and Understanding, **4** marks)

(b)   Study the Source below, then answer the question which follows.

The results of the 1997 General Election in Scotland

Party	% of vote gained using First Past The Post	Number of seats won using First Past The Post	Number of seats won if Proportional Representation was used
Labour	45	56	32
Conservative	18	0	13
Liberal Democrat	13	10	9
SNP	22	6	16
Other	2	0	2
Totals	100	72	72

Source: *The Independent*, May 1997

> "The present system of First Past The Post is good for the Conservative Party and fair for the voters of Scotland."

Conservative Party spokesperson

Using only the Source above, give **two** reasons why the Conservative Party in Scotland should consider changing the voting system from First Past The Post to Proportional Representation.

(Enquiry Skills, **4** marks)

QUESTION 1 (CONTINUED)

(c)   Study the Source below, then answer the question which follows.

Number of women candidates and MPs in the UK (1987–1997)						
		Women MPs				Total MPs
Year	Women candidates	Conservative	Labour	Liberal Democrat	Others	
1987	327	17	21	2	1	41
1992	568	20	37	2	1	60
1997	372	13	101	3	3	120

Source: Politics Department, University of Stirling

What **two** conclusions can be reached about the ways in which the representation of women has changed since 1987?

Your answer must be based entirely on the Source above.

(Enquiry Skills, **4** marks)

(d)   Study the Source below, then answer the question which follows.

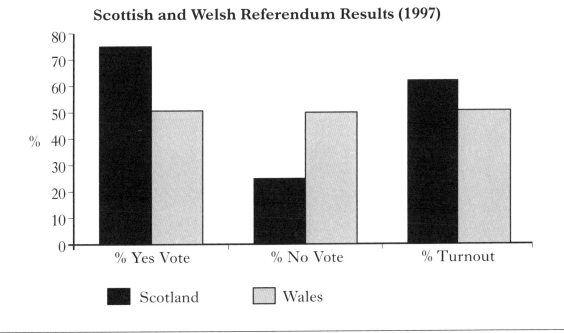

Scottish and Welsh Referendum Results (1997)

Scotland   Wales

"In the 1997 referendums in Scotland and Wales a large majority of voters in both countries voted yes. However, it was disappointing that only half the voters bothered to turn out to vote in both Scotland and Wales."

John Airlie

Using only the Source above, give **two** reasons why John Airlie could be accused of **exaggeration**.

(Enquiry Skills, **4** marks)

SYLLABUS AREA 2—CHANGING SOCIETY

QUESTION 2

(*a*)

> *Some families receive more financial help from the Government than others.*

Give **two** detailed reasons to explain why *some families receive more financial help from the Government than others.*

(Knowledge and Understanding, **4** marks)

(*b*)   Study Sources 1 and 2 below, then answer the question which follows.

SOURCE 1

Factfile on the Work of the Child Support Agency

- The Child Support Agency aims to make absent parents pay maintenance towards the cost of looking after their children.

- In its first two years, the Child Support Agency dealt with 1·25 million cases of children living with single parents.

- Since the Child Support Agency was set up, more than 15 000 single parent families have stopped receiving Income Support because the Government now believes they have enough money to live on.

Source: One Parent Families (Scotland) Website

SOURCE 2

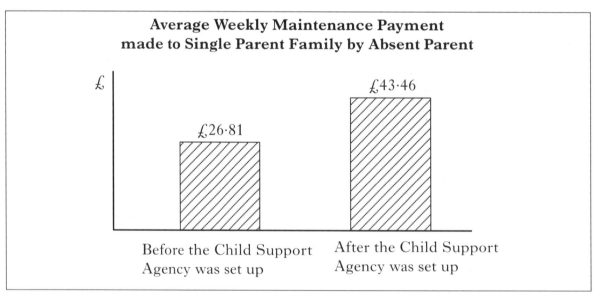

Average Weekly Maintenance Payment made to Single Parent Family by Absent Parent

Source: One Parent Families (Scotland) Website

> "The Child Support Agency has not reduced the number of single parent families receiving benefits. Families are no better off under the Child Support Agency than they were before."

Fiona Anderson

Using Sources 1 and 2 above, give **two** reasons why Fiona Anderson could be accused of **exaggeration**.

Your answer must be based on information from **both** Sources above.

(Enquiry Skills, **4** marks)

QUESTION 2 (CONTINUED)

(c)

> *Elderly people make more use of medical services than other age groups.*

Give **two** detailed reasons why *elderly people make more use of medical services than other age groups.*

(Knowledge and Understanding, **4** marks)

(d)   Study the plan of Stoneybridge below, then answer the question which follows.

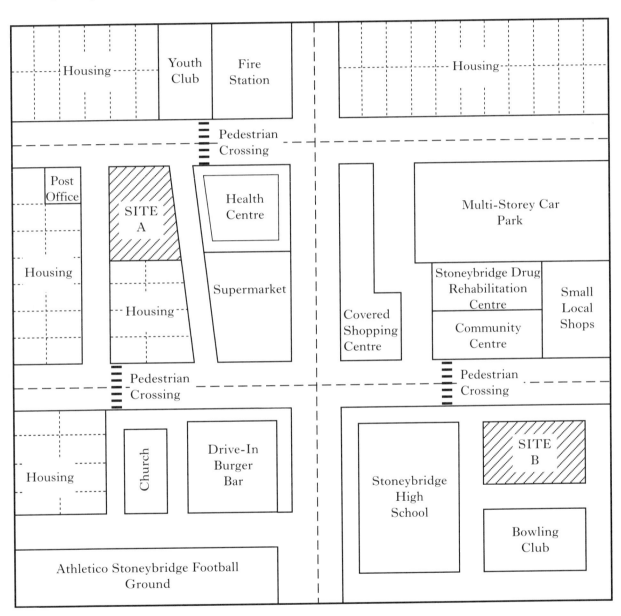

A building firm is intending to start work on a development of houses designed specially for elderly people. There are two areas of land available in Stoneybridge. They are undecided which to choose—**Site A or Site B**.

Using the information in the plan above, decide which site, **A or B**, would be the **better** place to build the houses for elderly people.

Give **two** reasons to support your decision.

Your answer must be based only on information from the plan above.

(Enquiry Skills, **4** marks)

SYLLABUS AREA 3—IDEOLOGIES

QUESTION 3

Answer **ONE** section only: Section (A)—The USA on pages six and seven

OR Section (B)—Russia on pages eight and nine

OR Section (C)—China on pages ten and eleven

(A) **THE USA**

(*a*)

> "Elections are important because they *allow American citizens to* **participate** *in choosing their* local and national *political representatives.*"

Statement by USA Citizen

Describe in detail the ways in which elections in the USA *allow American citizens to* **participate** *in choosing their political representatives.*

(Your answer must clearly refer to American political institutions and representatives.)

(Knowledge & Understanding, **4** marks)

(*b*)

> "In the USA, citizens and the media, including newspapers and television, have the right to criticise the government."

Statement by Newspaper Editor

Explain why most Americans think citizens and the media should have the right to criticise the Government.

Give **two** detailed reasons in your answer.

(Knowledge and Understanding, **4** marks)

QUESTION 3(A) (CONTINUED)

(c)

> **You are to investigate the issue of equal opportunities in the USA.**

(i)   As part of the Planning stage of your investigation, give **one** relevant aim/heading for your investigation into the issue of equal opportunities in the USA.

*(Enquiry Skills, **2** marks)*

(ii)   You decide to send a letter to the US Embassy* in London as part of your investigation into the issue of equal opportunities in the USA.

Explain why you have chosen this method of enquiry.

*(Enquiry Skills, **2** marks)*

The Ambassador
U.S. Embassy
Grosvenor Square
London

(iii) As part of the Collecting stage for your investigation, you send a letter to the US Embassy.

Give **two** relevant questions that you could include in your letter which would help you in your investigation into the issue of equal opportunities in the USA.

*(Enquiry Skills, **4** marks)*

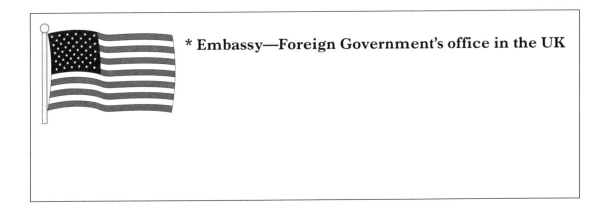

* **Embassy—Foreign Government's office in the UK**

NOW GO TO QUESTION 4 ON PAGE TWELVE

QUESTION 3 (CONTINUED)

(B) **RUSSIA**

(*a*)

"Elections are important as they allow Russian citizens to ***participate*** *in choosing their political representatives.*"

Statement by a Russian Journalist

Describe in detail **two** ways in which Russian citizens can ***participate*** *in choosing their political representatives.*

(Your answer must clearly refer to Russian political institutions and representatives.)

(Knowledge & Understanding, **4** marks)

(*b*)

"In Russia, the Government now has *less control over the media*, including newspapers and television."

Statement by a Newspaper Editor

Explain why most Russian citizens think that the government should have *less control over the media*.

Give **two** detailed reasons in your answer.

(Knowledge and Understanding, **4** marks)

QUESTION 3(B) (CONTINUED)

(c)

You are to investigate the issue of equal opportunities in Russia.

(i)   As part of the Planning stage of your investigation, give **one** relevant aim/heading for your investigation into the issue of equal opportunities in Russia.

(Enquiry Skills, **2** marks)

(ii)   You decide to send a letter to the Russian Embassy* in London as part of your investigation into the issue of equal opportunities in Russia.

Explain why you have chosen this method of enquiry.

(Enquiry Skills, **2** marks)

(iii) As part of the Collecting stage for your investigation, you send a letter to the Russian Embassy.

Give **two** relevant questions that you could include in your letter which would help you in your investigation into the issue of equal opportunities in Russia.

(Enquiry Skills, **4** marks)

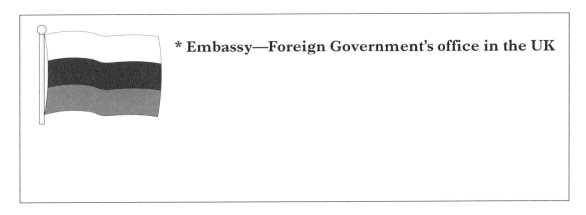

NOW GO TO QUESTION 4 ON PAGE TWELVE

QUESTION 3 (CONTINUED)

(C) **CHINA**

(*a*)

> "Elections are important because they allow citizens to **participate** *fully in choosing their government*."

Yung Lin a Democracy Campaigner

Explain in detail **two** reasons why Chinese citizens **cannot** *participate* *fully in choosing their government*.

(Your answer must clearly refer to the Chinese political system and institutions.)

(Knowledge & Understanding, 4 marks)

(*b*)

> "In China, the media, including newspapers and television, are controlled by the government."

Statement by a TV Producer

Explain why many Chinese citizens think the government should **not** control the media in China.

Give **two** detailed reasons in your answer.

(Knowledge & Understanding, 4 marks)

QUESTION 3(C) (CONTINUED)

(c)

> **You are to investigate the issue of equal opportunities in China.**

(i) As part of the Planning stage of your investigation, give **one** relevant aim/heading for your investigation into the issue of equal opportunities in China.

(Enquiry Skills, **2** marks)

(ii) You decide to send a letter to the Chinese Embassy* in London as part of your investigation into the issue of equal opportunities in China.

Explain why you have chosen this method of enquiry.

(Enquiry Skills, **2** marks)

(iii) As part of the Collecting stage for your investigation, you send a letter to the Chinese Embassy.

Give **two** relevant questions that you could include in your letter which would help you in your investigation into the issue of equal opportunities in China.

(Enquiry Skills, **4** marks)

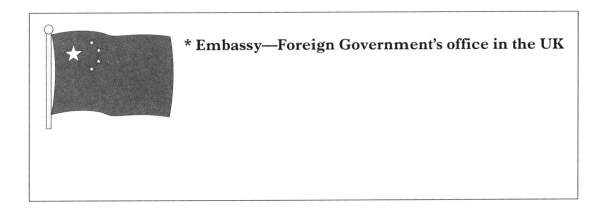

* Embassy—Foreign Government's office in the UK

NOW GO TO QUESTION 4 ON PAGE TWELVE

[Turn over

SYLLABUS AREA 4—INTERNATIONAL RELATIONS

QUESTION 4

(a) Study Sources 1 and 2 below, then answer the question which follows.

SOURCE 1

EU spending 1997 (%)

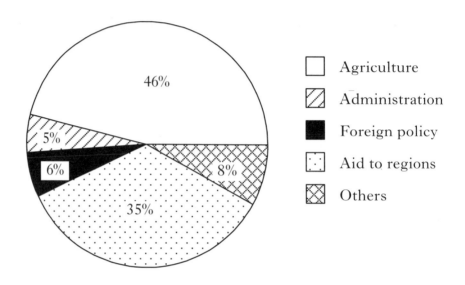

SOURCE 2

EU spending on agriculture 1993–99
(in European Currency Units)

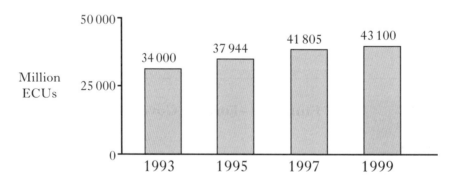

Source: Adapted from Europe in the Round, CD-ROM

> Spending on agriculture in the European Union (EU) costs far too much and the cost is still going up.

View of a Member of the European Parliament

Give **two** pieces of evidence to support the view of the European MP. Your reasons must be based on **both** Sources above.

(Enquiry Skills, **4** marks)

SYLLABUS AREA 4—INTERNATIONAL RELATIONS

QUESTION 4 (CONTINUED)

(b)

> Fifteen countries are now members of the European Union (EU). Other countries wish to join the EU.

Describe in detail **two** ways in which a country can benefit from being a member of the European Union.

(Knowledge & Understanding, **4** marks)

(c)   Study Sources 1 and 2 below, then answer the question which follows.

SOURCE 1	**SOURCE 2**
Changes affecting NATO	**Changes to NATO's forces**
USSR and the Warsaw Pact have collapsed; Russia is no longer an enemy	Large reduction in force numbers; many US troops have left Europe
Russia has scrapped many nuclear and other weapons	Reduction in nuclear missiles, tanks and guns
Terrorism is still a threat	Increased use of helicopters and transport aircraft to move rapid reaction forces
Peacekeeping forces are needed in Bosnia and may be needed in other parts of Eastern Europe	Building more aircraft carriers and landing craft
Forces are needed to serve outwith Europe, for example in the Middle East	Increased training for special forces, for example commandos

Give **two** conclusions that can be made about the ways in which changes affecting NATO have led to changes in NATO forces. Your answer must be based entirely on the Sources above.

(Enquiry Skills, **4** marks)

(d)

> Most of the countries in Eastern Europe want *to become members of the NATO alliance.*

Describe in detail **two** advantages for countries in Eastern Europe if they are allowed *to become members of the NATO alliance.*

(Knowledge & Understanding, **4** marks)

[END OF QUESTION PAPER]

[BLANK PAGE]

2640/402

NATIONAL QUALIFICATIONS 2000	THURSDAY, 8 JUNE G/C 9.00 AM – 10.30 AM F/G 10.20 AM – 11.50 AM	MODERN STUDIES STANDARD GRADE General Level

1   Read every question carefully.

2   Answer all questions as fully as you can.

3   If you cannot do a question, go on to the next one. Try again later.

4   In question 3, answer **one** section only.

5   Write your answers in the answer book provided. Indicate clearly, in the left hand margin, the question and section of question being answered. Do not write in the right hand margin.

SCOTTISH QUALIFICATIONS AUTHORITY

SYLLABUS AREA 1—LIVING IN A DEMOCRACY

QUESTION 1

(a)

> "Trade Unions *represent their members* in several different ways."

Describe **two** ways in which Trade Unions **represent** their members.

(Knowledge and Understanding, **4** marks)

(b)   Study Sources 1 and 2 below, then answer the question which follows.

SOURCE 1

UNISON

Members: 1 368 796

Male: 402 426   Female: 966 370

People represented: workers in local government, health care, higher education, transport, water, gas and electricity.

SOURCE 2

MUSICIANS UNION (MU)

Members: 33 134

Male: 30 990   Female: 2144

People represented: people within the music profession.

> "All Trade Unions are the same."

Jane Ferguson

Using the information in Sources 1 and 2 above, give **two** reasons why Jane Ferguson could be accused of **exaggeration**.

Your answer must be based entirely on the Sources above.

(Enquiry Skills, **4** marks)

QUESTION 1 (CONTINUED)

(c)

**LOCAL PEOPLE
OPPOSE NEW
MOTORWAY PLAN**

Describe **one right** and **one responsibility** that people have when they oppose a plan such as the building of a new motorway.

(Knowledge and Understanding, **4** marks)

(d)   Study the information below, then answer the question which follows.

Reasons for Voting for a Political Party	1992 %	1997 %
Agree with party policies	37	45
Usually vote for that party	20	20
Dislike other parties	22	13
Like the party leader	5	9
Good local candidate	7	4
Other reasons	9	9

Comparing the figures for 1992 and 1997, write down **two conclusions** that can be drawn about the changes in the reasons for voting for a political party.

Your answer must be based entirely on the information above.

(Enquiry Skills, **4** marks)

[Turn over

SYLLABUS AREA 2—CHANGING SOCIETY

QUESTION 2

(a)

> The Labour Government has policies to *help the unemployed and people in low paid work*.

Describe **two** ways in which the policies of the Labour Government *help the unemployed and people in low paid work*.

(Knowledge and Understanding, **4** marks)

(b)   Choose **one** of the following groups.

Disabled	:	**Ethnic Minorities**	:	**Older Workers**

Give **two** reasons why the group you have chosen may have difficulties in finding a job.

(Knowledge and Understanding, **4** marks)

QUESTION 2 (CONTINUED)

You are investigating the issue in the box below.

Answer the three questions (*c*), (*d*) and (*e*) which follow.

Living standards for different types of family

(*c*) As part of the Planning Stage, give **one** relevant aim or heading for this investigation.

(Enquiry Skills, **2** marks)

(*d*) You have decided to **interview** a spokesperson from the local branch of the Child Poverty Action Group.

Give **one** reason to explain why an **interview** is a good method of enquiry for this investigation.

(Enquiry Skills, **2** marks)

(*e*) Give **two** relevant questions which you could include in your **interview** that would help you with this investigation.

(Enquiry Skills, **4** marks)

[Turn over

SYLLABUS AREA 3—IDEOLOGIES

QUESTION 3

Answer **ONE** section only: Section (A)—The USA on pages six and seven

                            OR Section (B)—Russia on pages eight and nine

                            OR Section (C)—China on pages ten and eleven

(A) THE USA

(*a*)

> There are many ways in which people can *participate in politics* in the USA.

Apart from voting, describe **two** ways in which Americans can ***participate*** *in politics*. Your answer should refer to the USA.

(Knowledge & Understanding, **4** marks)

(*b*)   Study the information below, then answer the question which follows.

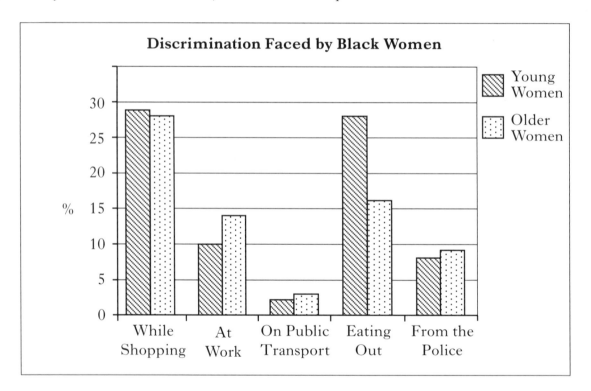

Discrimination Faced by Black Women

> "Young black women experience more discrimination than older black women."

View of Sheivon Murphy

Using only the information above, give **two** pieces of evidence to support the view of Sheivon Murphy.

(Enquiry Skills, **4** marks)

QUESTION 3(A) (CONTINUED)

(c)

> "*Some Americans have higher living standards than others.*"

Give **two** reasons why *some Americans have higher living standards than others.*

(Knowledge and Understanding, **4** marks)

(d)   Study Sources 1 and 2 below, then answer the question which follows.

SOURCE 1	SOURCE 2

AMERICA IS BETTER WITH THE DEMOCRATS

As **Democrats** we want to:

- Have tighter controls on pollution to protect the environment
- Have a strong foreign policy to keep America as a powerful country
- Make sure that the American Dream is available for all
- Look at ways of making Gun Laws safer.

REPUBLICANS ARE BEST FOR THE USA

As **Republicans** we want to:

- Increase the number of Americans achieving the American Dream
- Protect the rights of all Americans to own guns
- Keep the present laws on pollution to protect the rights of businesses
- Keep America's position as one of the most powerful countries in the world.

> "There are no similarities between the policies of the Democrats and the Republicans."

Hunter McCartney

Using only Sources 1 and 2 above, give **two** reasons why Hunter McCartney could be accused of **exaggeration**.

(Enquiry Skills, **4** marks)

NOW GO TO QUESTION 4 ON PAGE TWELVE

QUESTION 3 (CONTINUED)

(B) RUSSIA

(a)

> "There are many ways in which people can *participate in politics* in Russia."

Apart from voting, describe **two** ways that Russians can ***participate*** *in politics.*
Your answer should refer to Russia.

(Knowledge & Understanding, **4** marks)

(b) Study the information below, then answer the question which follows.

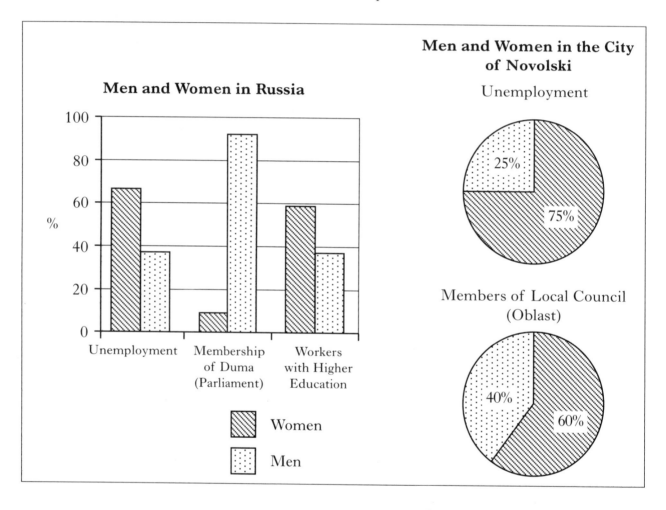

> "Compared to men, women in Russia suffer disadvantage."

View of Nikita Pavlov

Using only the information above, give **two** pieces of evidence to **support** the view of Nikita Pavlov.

(Enquiry Skills, **4** marks)

QUESTION 3(B) (CONTINUED)

(c)

> *"Some Russians have higher living standards than others."*

Give **two** reasons why *some Russians have higher living standards than others.*

(Knowledge and Understanding, **4** marks)

(d)   Study Sources 1 and 2 below, then answer the question which follows.

SOURCE 1   SOURCE 2

COMMUNISTS CARE!	

As **Communists** we want:

* To improve the living standards of all Russians

* To govern Russia through democratic methods

* To make the Government in Moscow more powerful

* To expand our industries.

THE PEOPLE'S PARTY	

As **Liberal Democrats** we want:

* To improve democracy throughout Russia

* To give more power to Local Governments throughout Russia

* To improve the economy and living standards

* To control industry and reduce pollution.

> "There are no similarities between the policies of the Communists and the Liberal Democrats in Russia."

View of Mikhail Khodovsky

Using only Sources 1 and 2 above, give **two** reasons why Mikhail Khodovsky could be accused of **exaggeration**.

(Enquiry Skills, **4** marks)

NOW GO TO QUESTION 4 ON PAGE TWELVE

QUESTION 3 (CONTINUED)

(C) CHINA

(a)

"There are several *ways in which people can participate in politics in China*."

Apart from voting, describe **two** *ways in which people can* **participate** *in politics in China.*

Your answer should refer to China.

(Knowledge & Understanding, **4** marks)

(b)   Study the information below, then answer the question which follows.

Male and Female—Contrasts in Jobs

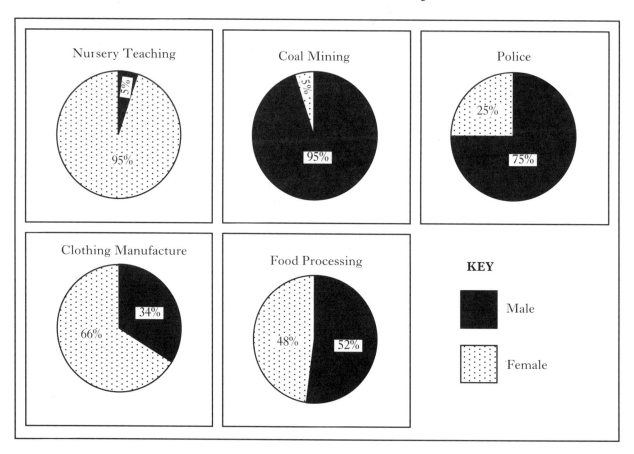

"A smaller percentage of women than men are employed in all jobs in China."

View of Katherine Fok Lo

Using only the information above, give **two** pieces of evidence to **support** the view of Katherine Fok Lo.

(Enquiry Skills, **4** marks)

QUESTION 3(C) (CONTINUED)

(c)

> "Some Chinese people have higher living standards than others."

Give **two** reasons why *some Chinese people have higher living standards than others*.

(Knowledge and Understanding, **4** marks)

(d) Study Sources 1 and 2 below, then answer the question which follows.

SOURCE 1   **SOURCE 2**

A BETTER CHINA THROUGH COMMUNISM!

We are the governing **Communist Party** and we want:

- Tibet to remain as part of China
- To punish severely all anti-social elements in China
- Macau to follow Hong Kong and be returned to Chinese ownership
- Careful attention to be paid to the environment to prevent unnecessary pollution.

CHINA FOR CHANGE!

We are **dissidents**, opponents of the Communist Party and we want:

- To free all political prisoners and hold proper elections
- More importance given to looking after the environment of China
- The island of Macau to be returned to China
- Newspapers and television to be free of all Government control.

> "There are no similarities between the views of the Government and dissident groups in China."

View of Chen Zihua

Using only Sources 1 and 2 above, give **two** reasons why Chen Zihua could be accused of **exaggeration**.

(Enquiry Skills, **4** marks)

NOW GO TO QUESTION 4 ON PAGE TWELVE

[Turn over

SYLLABUS AREA 4—INTERNATIONAL RELATIONS

QUESTION 4

(*a*)   Study the information below, then answer the question which follows.

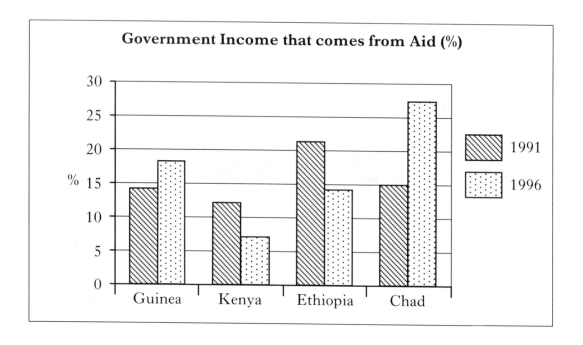

Government Income that comes from Aid (%)

Statements made in a speech by Ian Thomson, Aid Officer

- All four African countries have seen a reduction in the percentage of their government income that comes from aid.

- In 1991 Ethiopia relied most heavily on aid.

- By 1996 Chad relied most heavily on aid.

- In Kenya the percentage of government income coming from aid has remained the same.

Using the information above, write down **two** statements made by Ian Thomson which are **exaggerated**.

Using the bar graph, give a **reason** why **each** of the statements you have chosen is **exaggerated**.

(Enquiry Skills, **4** marks)

SYLLABUS AREA 4—INTERNATIONAL RELATIONS

QUESTION 4 (CONTINUED)

(b)   Study the profile below, then answer the question which follows.

Profile of Cameroon and Cote d'Ivoire

Country	Percentage of population with access to safe water	Percentage of national wealth spent on health	Infant Death Rate (per 1000 live births)	Percentage of children suffering malnutrition
Cameroon	41%	1·0%	54	15%
Cote d'Ivoire	72%	1·4%	84	24%

Using the table above, say which of the two countries should receive aid.

Give **two** reasons to **support** your answer.

Your answer must be based entirely on the profile above.

(Enquiry Skills, **4** marks)

(c)

> Aid organisations support projects that aim to *meet the needs of the poorest people in Africa.*

Describe **two** aid projects that would help *meet the **needs** of the poorest people in Africa.*

In your answer, give examples from countries you have studied.

(Knowledge and Understanding, **4** marks)

[Turn over for Question 4(d) on Page *fourteen*

SYLLABUS AREA 4—INTERNATIONAL RELATIONS

QUESTION 4 (CONTINUED)

(d)   Study the Sources below then answer the question which follows.

SOURCE 1

Background to War in Sierra Leone

The people of Sierra Leone, a country in West Africa, are split into two groups—those from the capital city (Freetown) and those from the countryside.

Those who live in the capital city, Freetown, and along the coast, have always been better off. They have formed the most powerful group in the country. Most members of the government come from this group.

The rebels who are fighting the government are supported by people from the countryside. They are poorer than the people in the cities. They have little say in Government.

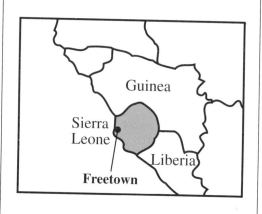

SOURCE 2

NEWSPAPER REPORT

President Kabbah of Sierra Leone wants the United Nations to act against foreign arms suppliers. Foreign countries have sold weapons to the rebels in Sierra Leone. This makes the conflict more difficult to bring to an end.

In a nationwide television broadcast, President Kabbah appealed to foreign countries to stop selling weapons to the rebels. This would give the country a chance of rebuilding its economy.

Source: Adapted from BBC News Website

"Foreign countries are to blame for the conflict in Sierra Leone."

View of Independent Observer

Give **one** reason to **support** the view and **one** to **oppose** the view of the Independent Observer. Your reasons must be based entirely on evidence from Sources 1 and 2 above.

(Enquiry Skills, **4** marks)

[END OF QUESTION PAPER]

G

2640/402

NATIONAL
QUALIFICATIONS
2001

FRIDAY, 1 JUNE
G/C   9.00 AM – 10.30 AM
F/G 10.20 AM – 11.50 AM

MODERN STUDIES
STANDARD GRADE
General Level

1   Read every question carefully.

2   Answer all questions as fully as you can.

3   If you cannot do a question, go on to the next one. Try again later.

4   In question 3, answer **one** section only.

5   Write your answers in the answer book provided. Indicate clearly, in the left hand margin, the
question and section of question being answered. Do not write in the right hand margin.

SCOTTISH
QUALIFICATIONS
AUTHORITY

SYLLABUS AREA 1—LIVING IN A DEMOCRACY

QUESTION 1

(a)

> Scottish voters are **represented** by Members of the Scottish Parliament (MSPs).

Describe **two** ways in which MSPs can **represent** people who live in their area.

(Knowledge and Understanding, **4** marks)

(b)   Study the table below, then answer the question which follows.

Election Results for the Scottish Parliament in the Ayr Constituency		
Party	*% of Vote May 1999*	*% of Vote March 2000*
Labour	38	22
Conservative	38	39
SNP	19	29
Lib Dem	4	3
Others	0	7

Write down **two** conclusions that can be reached about **the support for political parties** when the results of the two elections are compared.

Your answer must be based entirely on information from the table above.

(Enquiry Skills, **4** marks)

QUESTION 1 (CONTINUED)

You are investigating the topic in the box below.

> **Methods used by members of a Pressure Group during a campaign to improve road safety.**

Answer questions (c), (d) and (e) which follow.

(c) As part of the Planning Stage, give **two** relevant aims or headings for your investigation.

(Enquiry Skills, **2** marks)

(d) You have decided to **write a letter** to the Pressure Group, asking about the methods used in its campaign.

Give **one** reason why **writing a letter** is a good method of enquiry for your investigation.

(Enquiry Skills, **2** marks)

(e) Give **two** relevant questions which you could include in your **letter**.

(Enquiry Skills, **4** marks)

[Turn over

SYLLABUS AREA 2—CHANGING SOCIETY

QUESTION 2

(a)   Describe **two** ways in which sheltered housing meets the **needs** of some elderly people.

(Knowledge and Understanding, **4** marks)

(b)   Study Sources 1 and 2 below, then answer the question that follows.

SOURCE 1

% of Elderly Population by Gender			
	60–74	75–84	Over 85
Male	41%	33%	24%
Female	59%	67%	76%

SOURCE 2

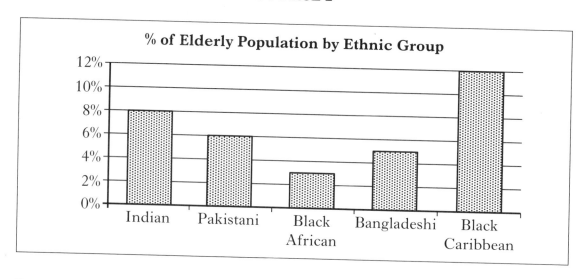

% of Elderly Population by Ethnic Group

"The percentage of elderly in the UK is increasing. There are more elderly men than women. All ethnic groups have a similar percentage of elderly people. The elderly have many needs."

View of Government spokesperson

Using Sources 1 and 2 above, give **two** reasons why the Government spokesperson could be accused of **exaggeration**.

Your answer must be based entirely on the sources above.

(Enquiry Skills, **4** marks)

QUESTION 2 (CONTINUED)

(c)

> *Some elderly people are wealthier than others.*

Give **two** reasons why *some elderly people are wealthier than others.*

(Knowledge and Understanding, **4** marks)

(d)   Study Sources 1 and 2 below, then answer the question which follows.

SOURCE 1

Daily Reporter: Shock Report on Child Poverty

The average income of all families has risen by 44%. There has been an increase of 70% in the income of the richest families, but the average income of the poorest families dropped by 10%. The Government must act urgently to ensure that all children in the UK have access to a decent standard of living.

Adapted from various sources

SOURCE 2

% of Children Living in Poverty in Europe	
Denmark	5%
France	12%
Germany	13%
Ireland	28%
Italy	24%
UK	32%

Eurostat figures

> "Poverty is a major problem in the UK."

View of Children's Charity worker

Using only Sources 1 and 2, give **two** reasons to support the view of the charity worker.

Your answer must be based entirely on the sources above.

(Enquiry Skills, **4** marks)

[Turn over

SYLLABUS AREA 3—IDEOLOGIES

QUESTION 3

Answer **ONE** section only: Section (A)—The USA on pages six and seven

                                 OR Section (B)—Russia on pages eight and nine

                                 OR Section (C)—China on pages ten and eleven

(A) THE USA

(a)

> *People in the USA can try to influence decisions made by their government.*

Apart from voting, describe **two** ways in which *people in the USA can try to influence decisions made by their government.*

In your answer you must refer to USA examples.

(Knowledge & Understanding, **4** marks)

(b)   Study Sources 1 and 2 below, then answer the question which follows.

SOURCE 1   **SOURCE 2**

The Constitution makes sure that the USA has a good human rights record. The second amendment says it is the right of American people to own guns. They need them for hunting and to protect their families.

The Supreme Court protects the human rights of the American people. It has allowed the death penalty since 1976.

The death penalty is a good punishment for people who commit very serious crimes. Criminals deserve to be put to death if they have killed innocent people.

Joe Barnes

There have been over 600 executions in the USA since 1976. Many states still use the death penalty.

The death penalty is wrong for any crime—even a serious one such as murder. I feel that an innocent person could be found guilty and given the death penalty.

The human rights record of the USA is terrible for a civilised country. People can easily own guns and innocent people are often attacked. The USA must protect the innocent victims and stop young people from having the right to own guns.

Odell Diamond

Sources 1 and 2 give different views about human rights in the USA.

What are **two** of the differences between these views?

(Enquiry Skills, **4** marks)

(c)

> Many people believe that *the economic system of the USA works well.*

Give **two** reasons to explain why many people believe that *the economic system of the USA works well.*

(Knowledge & Understanding, **4** marks)

QUESTION 3(A) (CONTINUED)

(d)   Study Sources 1 and 2 below, then answer the question which follows.

SOURCE 1

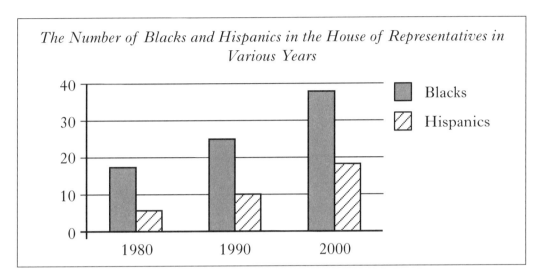

The Number of Blacks and Hispanics in the House of Representatives in Various Years

Adapted from various Internet sites

SOURCE 2

Black employment and home ownership are increasing. The percentage of black families living below the poverty line is at its lowest since 1967. Even black men with poor qualifications have better job prospects. There are now six times as many black elected officials as there were in 1970. There are 9000—the highest number ever.

However, times are not good for all blacks. More black men than ever are in prison. Black success in education still falls behind that of whites. Suicides among young black men have risen sharply, reflecting a sense of hopelessness.

Adapted from Newsweek, 7/6/99

"The situation of Blacks in the USA is not improving."

View of Lyz Smith

Using Sources 1 and 2 above, give **two** reasons why Lyz Smith could be accused of **exaggeration**.

Your answer must be based on information from both Sources 1 and 2.

(Enquiry Skills, **4** marks)

NOW GO TO QUESTION 4 ON PAGE TWELVE

QUESTION 3 (CONTINUED)

(B) **RUSSIA**

(a)

> *People in Russia can try to influence decisions made by their government.*

Apart from voting, describe **two** ways in which *people in Russia can try to influence decisions made by their government.*

In your answer you must refer to Russian examples.

(Knowledge & Understanding, **4** marks)

(b) Study Sources 1 and 2 below, then answer the question which follows.

<table>
<tr><th>SOURCE 1</th><th>SOURCE 2</th></tr>
<tr><td>

The rest of the world has a responsibility to draw attention to the problems of human rights in Russia. Many people are not given basic human rights.

During the recent war in Chechnya, many innocent Chechens were killed or injured by the Russian army. The war was one of the worst in Europe in the 1990s.

President Clinton of the USA and President Putin of Russia have met, but hardly spoke about human rights.

Helen Hudd
</td><td>

The leaders of Russia and the USA met to discuss economic problems. Human rights were hardly mentioned.

The Russian Army have been involved in a military campaign in Chechnya. They have been careful to target only terrorists—ordinary people have not been killed or injured.

Outsiders should not try to interfere with human rights in Russia. What happens in Russia is the responsibility of the Russian government.

Boris Bulganin
</td></tr>
</table>

Sources 1 and 2 give different views about human rights in Russia.

What are **two** of the differences between these views?

(Enquiry Skills, **4** marks)

(c)

> *Many people believe that the economic system of Russia does not work well.*

Give **two** reasons to explain why *many people believe that the economic system of Russia does not work well.*

(Knowledge & Understanding, **4** marks)

QUESTION 3(B) (CONTINUED)

(d)   Study Sources 1 and 2 below, then answer the question which follows.

SOURCE 1

Elections for the President of Russia are held every four years. Boris Yeltsin was the first President of Russia following the end of Communism. He was elected in 1992 and again in 1996.

In January 2000 an opinion poll gave Putin 35% of the support from the Russian people. By March 2000 this had increased to 53% with Zyuganov in second place with 24%. The two other candidates were well behind. Putin eventually won with a clear result. The turnout at the election was a disappointing 60%.

SOURCE 2

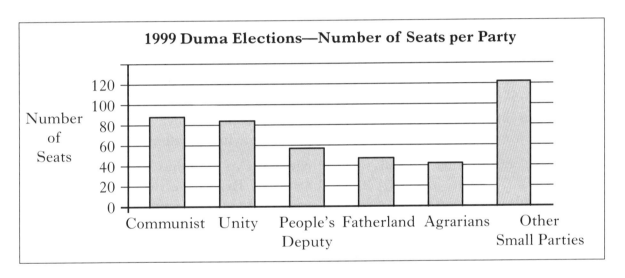

1999 Duma Elections—Number of Seats per Party

"Putin's support remained constant throughout the election campaign. The Unity Party and the Communist Party were delighted with the 1999 Duma elections."

View of Yevgeny Martinov

Using Sources 1 and 2 above, give **two** reasons why Yevgeny Martinov could be accused of **exaggeration**.

Your answer must be based on information from both Sources 1 and 2.

(Enquiry Skills, **4** marks)

NOW GO TO QUESTION 4 ON PAGE TWELVE

QUESTION 3 (CONTINUED)

(C) CHINA

(a)

> *People in China can try to influence decisions taken by their government.*

Apart from voting, describe **two** ways in which *people in China can try to influence decisions taken by their government.*

In your answer you must refer to Chinese examples.

(Knowledge & Understanding, **4** marks)

(b) Study Sources 1 and 2 below, then answer the question which follows.

SOURCE 1

In China, all citizens enjoy basic freedoms and human rights. These are written down in the Constitution of the country.

The government protects the religious freedom of its citizens. For example, there are about three thousand different religious groups in China, with a total membership of over 100 million.

Chinese people are entitled to feel safe from criminals. That is why the government hands out strong punishments to those who commit serious crimes.

Lee Deng Shek

SOURCE 2

China hands out severe sentences to people found guilty of serious crimes. Many Chinese people feel safe because of this.

However, there are many people in China who are unhappy with the government. These people believe that they are not given basic human rights.

Members of religious groups have been arrested. Recently sixteen church leaders were sent to prison camps.

Kim Cheng

Sources 1 and 2 give different views about human rights in China.

What are **two** of the differences between these views?

(Enquiry Skills, **4** marks)

(c)

> Many people believe that *the economic system of China works well.*

Give **two** reasons to explain why many people believe that *the economic system of China works well.*

(Knowledge & Understanding, **4** marks)

QUESTION 3(C) (CONTINUED)

(d)   Study Sources 1 and 2 below, then answer the question which follows.

SOURCE 1

> At present 99·9% of China's citizens aged 18 and above have the right to vote and stand as candidates at elections. Chinese citizens can vote for village committees, workplace representatives, provincial assemblies and delegates to the National People's Congress.
>
> The Communist Party has been in power since 1949. It has 58 million members and usually gets over 90% of the votes cast in elections. Apart from the Communist Party there are eight other official political parties in China.

Adapted from Chinese Embassy website

SOURCE 2

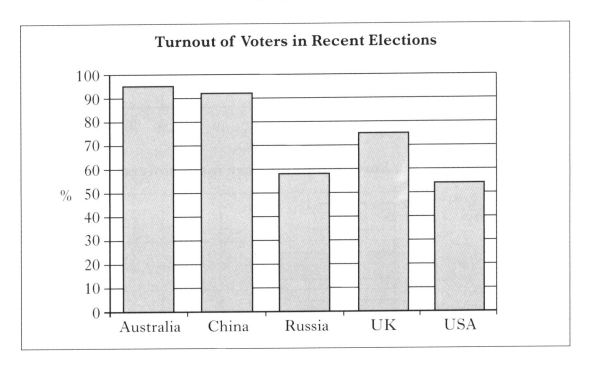

"Ordinary Chinese people do not get many opportunities to vote. When elections take place the turnout is low. There is more than one political party in China."

View of Ho Hun Yan

Using Sources 1 and 2 above, give **two** reasons why Ho Hun Yan could be accused of **exaggeration**.

Your answer must be based on information from both Sources 1 and 2.

(Enquiry Skills, **4** marks)

NOW GO TO QUESTION 4 ON PAGE TWELVE

SYLLABUS AREA 4—INTERNATIONAL RELATIONS

QUESTION 4

(a)

> NATO and the United Nations have been involved in the former Yugoslavia.

Describe **two** ways in which *NATO and the United Nations have been involved in the former Yugoslavia.*

(Knowledge and Understanding, **4** marks)

(b)   Study the information below, then answer the question which follows.

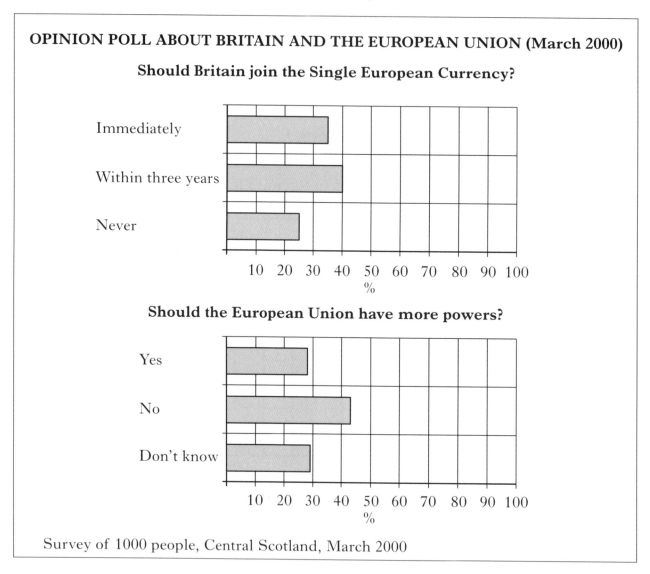

OPINION POLL ABOUT BRITAIN AND THE EUROPEAN UNION (March 2000)

Should Britain join the Single European Currency?

Should the European Union have more powers?

Survey of 1000 people, Central Scotland, March 2000

"Over half of the people surveyed in Central Scotland are in favour of Britain joining the Single European Currency before 2005. People also believe that the European Union should have more powers."

View of Tom McLeod, Member of the European Parliament

Using only the information above, give **one** piece of evidence to **support** and **one** piece of evidence to **oppose** the view of Tom McLeod.

(Enquiry Skills, **4** marks)

SYLLABUS AREA 4—INTERNATIONAL RELATIONS

QUESTION 4 (CONTINUED)

(c)

> The European Union meets the **needs** of people in Scotland.

Give **two** reasons to explain why many people believe that *the European Union meets the **needs** of people in Scotland.*

(Knowledge and Understanding, **4** marks)

(d)   Study the information below, then answer the question which follows.

Armed Forces of Selected NATO Members—Number of Troops (Thousands)			
	1995	*1996*	*1997*
UK	230	230	220
Germany	350	340	340
Turkey	800	800	820
USA	1620	1580	1550

Source: House of Commons Research Paper, 98/120

Study the information about the number of troops from selected NATO members.

Write down **two** conclusions that can be reached about **the changes that have taken place in the numbers of troops since 1995**.

Your answer must be based entirely on the information above.

(Enquiry Skills, **4** marks)

[END OF QUESTION PAPER]

[BLANK PAGE]

G

2640/402

NATIONAL
QUALIFICATIONS
2002

THURSDAY, 30 MAY
10.20 AM–11.50 AM

MODERN STUDIES
STANDARD GRADE
General Level

1   Read every question carefully.

2   Answer all questions as fully as you can.

3   If you cannot do a question, go on to the next one. Try again later.

4   In question 3, answer **one** section only.

5   Write your answers in the answer book provided. Indicate clearly, in the left hand margin, the question and section of question being answered. Do not write in the right hand margin.

SCOTTISH
QUALIFICATIONS
AUTHORITY

SYLLABUS AREA 1—LIVING IN A DEMOCRACY

QUESTION 1

(a)

> "More *members* should **take part** *in trade union activities.*"

Describe **two** ways in which *members* can **take part** *in trade union activities.*

(Knowledge and Understanding, **4** marks)

(b)   Study Sources 1 and 2 below, then answer the question which follows.

SOURCE 1

Women in UNISON

UNISON is an example of a Trade Union in which women are well-represented. 72% of the membership of UNISON is female, and the proportion has been increasing quickly over recent years.

The role of Trade Unions has changed over recent years. UNISON is concerned about issues such as education, child-care, racism and sexual harassment. More women are becoming involved in union activities and taking on positions as Union officials.

SOURCE 2

Women and the TGWU

The TGWU is one of the largest Unions in the country. 26% of its members are female—which is a big increase compared to a few years ago. Despite increasing numbers of female members, not many women have become Union officials.

Issues such as education, child-care, sexual harassment and racism are important for the TGWU. These used to be less important, but the work of Trade Unions has changed as time has passed.

Sources 1 and 2 give different views about the representation of women in trade unions.

Write down **two** of the differences between these views.

You must use only information from the Sources above.

(Enquiry Skills, **4** marks)

QUESTION 1 (CONTINUED)

(c)

> *People should use their **right** to vote.*

Give **two** reasons why *people should use their **right** to vote*.

(Knowledge and Understanding, **4** marks)

(d)   Study Sources 1 and 2 below, then answer the question which follows.

SOURCE 1

Typical Council Tax, 2001/2	
City of Edinburgh	£960
City of Glasgow	£1120
Scottish Borders	£785
Western Isles	£350

SOURCE 2

Extract from Radio News Broadcast

Council tax bills in Scotland increased by as much as 10% between 2000 and 2001. Council leaders have blamed the Scottish Executive for not giving them enough money to run services. However, some councils say that they will be able to increase spending on education and social work.

Services provided by some councils will improve next year. People in city areas will pay much more council tax than people in other areas.

View of Norman Anderson

Using **only** Sources 1 and 2, give **two** reasons to support the view of Norman Anderson.

You must use only information from the Sources above.

(Enquiry Skills, **4** marks)

[Turn over

SYLLABUS AREA 2—CHANGING SOCIETY

QUESTION 2

(*a*)   Study Sources 1 and 2 below, then answer the question that follows.

SOURCE 1

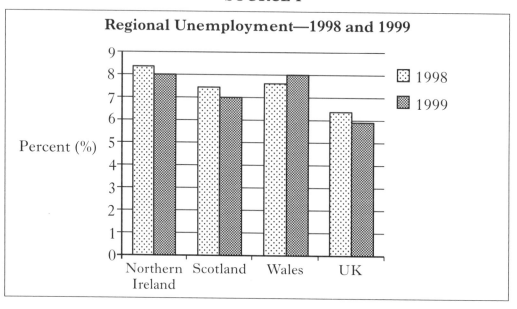

Regional Unemployment—1998 and 1999

SOURCE 2

Unemployment in Selected EU Countries—1999 (%)	
France	11·0
Germany	9·1
Italy	12·0
Netherlands	3·2
Portugal	4·8
Spain	15·6
Sweden	6·8
UK	5·9
EU Average	9·3

Scotland's unemployment rate is higher than the UK average. Unemployment in Scotland is increasing. The rate of unemployment in the UK is below the EU average. The Netherlands, Sweden and Portugal all have lower unemployment than the UK.

View of Opposition Spokesperson

Using **only** Sources 1 and 2 above, give **two** reasons why the Opposition Spokesperson could be accused of **exaggeration**.

You must use only information from the Sources above.

(Enquiry Skills, **4** marks)

QUESTION 2 CONTINUED)

(b)
> There are many ways that *the **needs** of unemployed people* can be met by the government.

Describe **two** ways in which the government helps meet *the **needs** of unemployed people*.

(Knowledge and Understanding, **4** marks)

(c)
> *Families with young children do not all have the same standard of living.*

Give **two** reasons why *families with young children do not all have the same standard of living*.

(Knowledge and Understanding, **4** marks)

(d)   Study the information below then answer the question which follows.

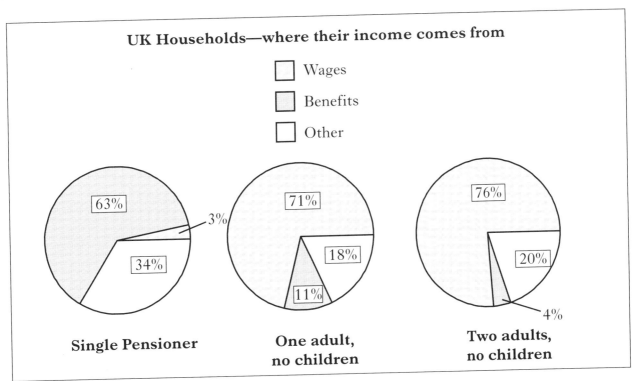

Write down **two** conclusions that can be reached about where different types of households get their income.

In your answer you should **compare different types of household**.

You must use only information from the Sources above.

(Enquiry Skills, **4** marks)

[Turn over

SYLLABUS AREA 3—IDEOLOGIES

QUESTION 3

Answer **ONE** section only: Section (A)—The USA on pages six to eight

                 OR Section (B)—Russia on pages nine to eleven

                 OR Section (C)—China on pages twelve to fourteen

(A) **THE USA**

(a)

Housing	Health	Crime and Justice

Choose **one** of the topics listed above.

Describe **two** ways in which some members of **ethnic minority groups** in the USA are not treated **equally** in the topic you have chosen.

In your answer you must refer to ethnic minorities in the USA that you have studied.

(Knowledge & Understanding, 4 marks)

(b)

Give **two** reasons why it is possible for some Americans to *become rich and successful*.

In your answer you must refer to American examples.

(Knowledge & Understanding, 4 marks)

QUESTION 3 (A) (CONTINUED)

(c)   Study Sources 1 and 2 below, then answer the question which follows.

SOURCE 1

The USA—Presidential Election 2000			
Candidate	Popular Votes	States Won*	Electoral College Votes
Gore (Democrat)	50·9 million	21	266
Bush (Republican)	50·4 million	30	271
Others	3·9 million	0	0

* includes Washington DC

SOURCE 2

Bush was elected President—Who did the people of the USA really want?

According to a CBS News poll, most Americans are satisfied with the outcome of the Presidential election. 55% said they were satisfied while 45% said they were not satisfied with the result.

Women of all races preferred Gore to Bush by 54% to 43%. Men, on the other hand, voted for Bush by 53% to 42%. A large majority of Black voters preferred Gore, while a small majority of White voters preferred Bush.

Most men are happy with the result of the 2000 Presidential election in the USA. The person with the most popular votes became President.

View of Eva Kaye, Florida voter

Using **only** Sources 1 and 2 above, give **one reason** to **support** and **one reason** to **oppose** the view of Eva Kaye.

You must use only information from the Sources above.

(Enquiry Skills, **4** marks)

[Turn over

QUESTION 3 (A) (CONTINUED)

(d)   Study Sources 1 and 2 below, then answer the question which follows.

SOURCE 1

Report in an American Newspaper

The **School Voucher Program** will allow parents to use taxpayers money to send their children to private schools instead of government-run schools.

The **School Voucher Program** will take money away from government-run schools and cause them huge problems. The **School Voucher Program** will hurt the very people it is meant to help—poor ethnic minority communities. Parents of able pupils will use these vouchers to pay for private education. This will leave government-run schools with even fewer resources and funds and cause even more problems for ethnic minorities.

SOURCE 2

Government-run Schools—Statistics			
	1992	*1996*	*2000*
On Internet (%)	20 (est)	65	97
Completing High School (%)			
All	79	82	84
White	83	86	89
Black	68	75	77
Hispanic	53	53	57

"The **School Voucher Program** allows parents to send their children to private schools. More pupils, of all ethnic groups, are completing High School. The School Voucher Program will benefit all pupils. Government-run schools do not have modern facilities like access to the Internet."

View of Jay Schulz

Using **only** Sources 1 and 2 above, give **two reasons** why Jay Schulz could be accused of **exaggeration**.

You must use only information from the Sources above.

(Enquiry Skills, **4** marks)

NOW GO TO QUESTION 4 ON PAGE FIFTEEN

QUESTION 3 (CONTINUED)

(B) RUSSIA

(a)

> Some *national groups within Russia are not treated fairly*.

Describe **two** ways in which some members of *national groups within Russia are not treated fairly*.

In your answer you must refer to national groups in Russia that you have studied.

(Knowledge & Understanding, **4** marks)

(b)

> *The Russian Government now encourages foreign businesses to open in places such as Moscow*.

Give **two** reasons why *the Russian Government now encourages foreign businesses to open in places such as Moscow*.

In your answer you must refer to specific examples.

(Knowledge & Understanding, **4** marks)

[Turn over

QUESTION 3 (B) (CONTINUED)

(c)   Study Sources 1 and 2 below, then answer the question which follows.

SOURCE 1

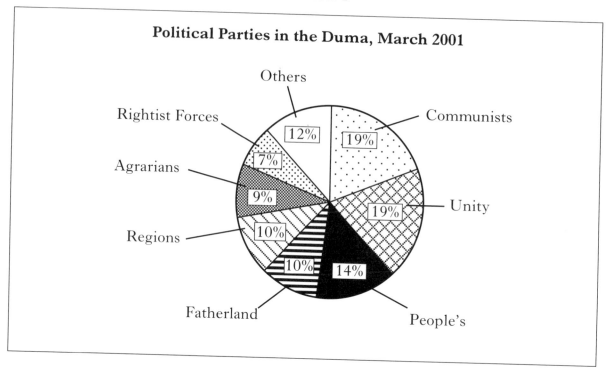

Political Parties in the Duma, March 2001

SOURCE 2

Vladimir Putin—The Man for Russia?

Vladimir Putin became President of the Russian Federation in March 2000. The previous President, Boris Yeltsin, had been in poor health for several years.

The election campaign was hard-fought, but Putin was always the favourite to win. He had been approved by Boris Yeltsin and had a spell in temporary charge of the country before the election took place. This was because Yeltsin was ill and it gave Putin the chance to prove he would be a good President. Putin gained 53% of the vote in the 2000 Presidential election, easily defeating his nearest rival Gennady Zyuganov. When the votes were counted Zyuganov had just under 30%.

> One party has an overall majority in the Duma. Vladimir Putin was a clear winner in the 2000 Presidential election.

View of Yevgeny Lovchev

Using **only** Sources 1 and 2 above, give **one reason** to **support** and **one reason** to **oppose** the view of Yevgeny Lovchev.

You must use only information from the Sources above.

(Enquiry Skills, **4** marks)

QUESTION 3(B) (CONTINUED)

(d)   Study Sources 1 and 2 below, then answer the question which follows.

SOURCE 1

Share of Total Employment in Russia, 1990 and 1998 (%): Selected Jobs		
Job Type	*1990*	*1998*
Industry	30·3	22·2
Agriculture and Fishing	13·2	13·0
Construction	12·0	8·5
Transport and Commerce	6·6	7·9
Retail	7·8	14·0
Housing	4·3	5·8

SOURCE 2

Letter to the Editor of a Russian Newspaper

Sir,

I am writing on behalf of the coal miners in the Vorkuta region of Northern Russia. The coal mines of our area produce huge amounts of coal that are vital to Russia's economy.

Due to poor management many of the miners have not been paid on a regular basis for several months now. Their families are suffering because of this situation. The government in Moscow must act now to make sure that essential workers are paid!

Yours in comradeship,

Vladimir Yuran

Jobs in industry are still the most important employment sector in Russia. The Construction industry has seen an increase in importance. All Russian workers are now paid on a regular basis. The coal miners of the Vorkuta region produce coal that is vital to the Russian economy.

View of Boris Demiananko

Using **only** Sources 1 and 2 above, give **two reasons** why Boris Demiananko could be accused of **exaggeration**.

You must use only information from the Sources above.

(Enquiry Skills, **4** marks)

NOW GO TO QUESTION 4 ON PAGE FIFTEEN

QUESTION 3 (CONTINUED)

(C) CHINA

(a)

> *People in some regions of China feel that they are not treated **equally**.*

Describe **two** ways in which *people in some regions of China feel that they are not treated **equally***.

In your answer you must refer to people from regions of China that you have studied.

(Knowledge and Understanding, **4** marks)

(b)

> *The Chinese government now encourages some foreign businesses to open in China.*

Give **two** reasons why *the Chinese government now encourages foreign businesses to open in China*.

In your answer you must refer to specific examples.

(Knowledge and Understanding, **4** marks)

QUESTION 3(C) (CONTINUED)

(c) Study Sources 1 and 2 below, then answer the question which follows.

SOURCE 1

Political Parties in China

Party	Membership
Communist Party	57 000 000
China Democratic League	105 000
China Democratic National Construction Association	50 000
China Association for Promoting Democracy	50 000
China Revolutionary Committee of the Kuomingtang	40 000
China Peasants and Workers Democratic Party	40 000
Jisuan Society	40 000
Chinese Party for the Public Interest	10 000

SOURCE 2

Communism at the Crossroads

The Chinese Communist Party celebrated its 80th anniversary on July 1st 2001. Some members remain loyal to the teachings of Mao Ze Dong and want no change to hard-line policies. Wang Chaglin, manager of a state company, has just set up the Mao Zedong Thought website and says it receives thousands of hits every day. Other members want to see the Chinese Communist Party become more modern. The 16th Communist Party Congress, due to take place in 2002, will see new leaders introduced and policy changes proposed.

The Communist Party is the largest political party in China. All members of the party agree on future policies.

View of Fan Zhiyi

Using **only** Sources 1 and 2 above, give **one reason** to **support** and **one reason** to **oppose** the view of Fan Zhiyi.

You must use only information from the Sources above.

(Enquiry Skills, **4** marks)

QUESTION 3 (C) (CONTINUED)

(d)   Study Sources 1 and 2 below then answer the question which follows.

SOURCE 1

April 1st

Collision between a Chinese fighter jet and an American spy plane aircraft. The Chinese pilot dies and the American crew are detained in China.

April 2nd

Investigation reveals that the Chinese jet rammed the spy plane, causing it to crash land. The Americans are denied access to the plane.

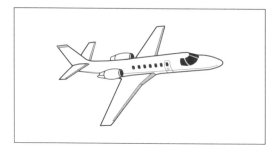

April 11th

The American crew are released. China still refuses to hand back the American aircraft.

April 6th

China is not happy that the Americans will not apologise.

SOURCE 2

Factfile

- The US military has spoken to China about five incidents in 2001 when Chinese planes came dangerously close to US flights.

- The US plane belonged to the navy and was on a routine flight above international waters.

- China is unhappy that the US is selling weapons to Taiwan.

The Chinese are correct to blame America for the incident. China is happy about American links with Taiwan.

View of Wan Zee

Using **only** Sources 1 and 2 above, give **two reasons** why Wan Zee could be accused of **exaggeration**.

You must use only information from the Sources above.

(Enquiry Skills, **4** marks)

NOW GO TO QUESTION 4 ON PAGE FIFTEEN

SYLLABUS AREA 4—INTERNATIONAL RELATIONS

QUESTION 4

(a)

> *"United Nations aid **meets the needs** of developing countries in Africa in a number of different ways."*

Describe **two** ways in which *United Nations aid **meets the needs** of developing countries in Africa.*

(Knowledge and Understanding, **4** marks)

(b)   Study the information below, then answer the question which follows.

Selected African Countries—A comparison of levels of development in four countries

	Average Income per head ($)	*% of adults who can Read and Write*	*Life Expectancy (Years)*
Sudan	940	46	57
Ethiopia	560	35	45
Kenya	1600	78	48
Gabon	6500	63	50

Source – CIA World Factbook 2000

Compare the information about the levels of development in the four countries.

Write down **two** conclusions that can be reached about the different levels of development in the four countries.

In your answer you must **compare the countries**.

You must use only the information above.

(Enquiry Skills, **4** marks)

[Turn over for Question 4 (c) to (e) on *Page sixteen*

QUESTION 4 (CONTINUED)

You are investigating the topic in the box below.

┌───┐
│ **UK aid to developing countries in Africa** │
└───┘

Answer questions (*c*), (*d*), and (*e*) which follow.

(*c*)   As part of the Planning Stage, give **two** relevant aims or headings for your investigation.

(Enquiry Skills, **2** marks)

(*d*)   You have decided to write a **letter** to the Minister for Overseas Development in the UK government as a means of finding relevant information.

Give **one** advantage and **one** disadvantage of writing a letter as a way of finding out information for your investigation.

(Enquiry Skills, **4** marks)

(*e*)   Give **two** relevant questions which you could include in your **letter**.

(Enquiry Skills, **2** marks)

[END OF QUESTION PAPER]

2640/103

SCOTTISH
CERTIFICATE OF
EDUCATION
1998

WEDNESDAY, 20 MAY
10.45 AM – 12.45 PM

MODERN STUDIES
STANDARD GRADE
Credit Level

1   Read every question carefully.

2   Answer all questions as fully as you can.

3   If you cannot do a question, go on to the next one. Try again later.

4   In question 3, answer **one** section only.

5   Write your answers in the answer book provided. Indicate clearly, in the left hand margin, the question and section of question being answered. Do not write in the right hand margin.

SCOTTISH
QUALIFICATIONS
AUTHORITY
©

SYLLABUS AREA 1—LIVING IN A DEMOCRACY

QUESTION 1

(a) Study Sources 1, 2, 3 and 4 below and opposite, then answer the question which follows.

SOURCE 1

The result of the 1997 General Election in Scotland and the UK				
Party	% of votes Scotland	Number of seats Scotland	% of votes UK	Number of seats UK
Labour	46	56	43	419
Conservative	18	0	31	165
Lib Dem	13	10	17	46
SNP	22	6	2	6
Others	1	0	7	23

SOURCE 2

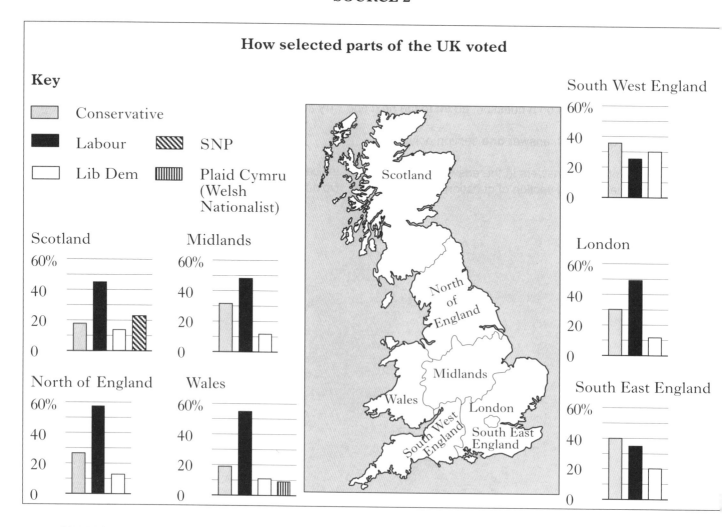

How selected parts of the UK voted

QUESTION 1 (CONTINUED)

SOURCE 3

Party support by sex and age (%)

	Conservative	Labour	Liberal Democrat
Men	31	44	17
Women	32	44	17
First time voters	19	57	18
Voters aged 65+	44	34	16

SOURCE 4

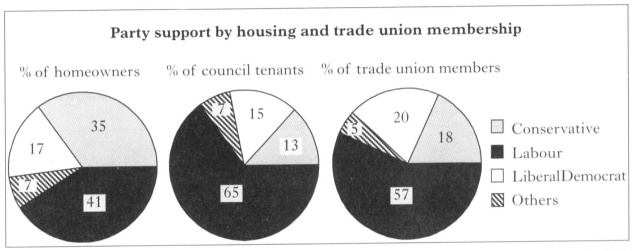

Party support by housing and trade union membership

% of homeowners   % of council tenants   % of trade union members

Conservative
Labour
LiberalDemocrat
Others

Sources: Adapted from *The Sunday Times*, May 1997 and the *Modern Studies Association Yearbook*, 1997

Using Sources 1, 2, 3 and 4 opposite and above, what conclusions can be drawn about support for the Labour Party in the 1997 General Election?

(Evaluating, **8** marks)

(b) "Newspapers and pressure groups have the right to try to influence political decisions in the UK. However, they have responsibilities as well as rights in the ways in which they can try to influence political decisions."

Choose **either** the newspapers **or** a pressure group.

Describe in detail **one right** and **one responsibility** the group you have chosen has when trying to influence political decisions in the UK.

(Knowledge & Understanding, **4** marks)

(c) "Elections for the new Scottish Parliament will involve a form of Proportional Representation."

Discuss the arguments **for** and **against** Proportional Representation.

(Knowledge & Understanding, **6** marks)

SYLLABUS AREA 2—CHANGING SOCIETY

QUESTION 2

(a)   Study Sources 1 and 2 below, then answer the question which follows.

SOURCE 1

Profile of Mrs Wilkie

The Social Work Department of her local council is trying to meet Mrs Wilkie's housing needs.

Personal details	Audrey Wilkie. Age 80. Widow with 2 grown-up children and 5 grandchildren—the nearest lives 75 miles away. She walks with a stick after breaking her leg last winter. Becoming slightly forgetful. Needs to be careful with her diet because of diabetes.
Present house	She lives alone in a council house with stairs and 2 bedrooms. She now finds using the stairs and cleaning the house difficult. Her rent is paid through Housing Benefit but she worries over heating costs.

SOURCE 2

OPTION A—Sheltered Housing

* Each resident lives in their own small flat with grab rails, ramped access, low worktops, high power points and phone.

* All flats are connected to an Emergency Alarm system. Residents push a button to call the Warden. Warden on duty 24-hours. Has First Aid Certificate.

* Communal lounge and recreation area with television, books and other hobbies.

* Bedrooms for visitors can be booked in advance.

OPTION B—Nursing Home

* 24-hour care and attention for residents—one trained nurse on duty at all times.

* All meals cooked and cleaning done for the residents. Individual menus prepared to suit residents.

* Regular visiting opportunities for families and friends of the residents.

* Each resident shares a bedroom, bath and toilet with one other person. Lounge facilities are shared. Access to television and telephone.

Using Sources 1 and 2 above, explain which of the two options **A** or **B** the Social Work Department should offer Mrs Wilkie.

Give reasons for your choice **and** say why you rejected the other option.

(Evaluating, **6** marks)

QUESTION 2 (CONTINUED)

(b)   Study Sources 3 and 4 below, then answer the question which follows.

SOURCE 3

Health problems and the elderly

	Age		
	65–74	75–84	85+
% unable to go out of doors alone	6	20	47
% unable to climb stairs without help	4	13	31
% unable to go to toilet without help	1	2	7
% unable to get into/out of bed without help	1	3	7

SOURCE 4

Percentage of over 65 year olds reporting long standing illness

Former occupation	Male	Female
Professional (eg lawyer/teacher)	49	61
Office workers	61	62
Factory workers	63	64

Source: General Household Survey

"A person's age, sex and former occupation have no effect on their health throughout their retirement."

Statement from politician

Using Sources 3 and 4 above, explain why the politician could be accused of being **selective** in the use of facts.

(Evaluating, **4** marks)

(c)

"*Medical technology has improved the lifestyles of many elderly people.*"

Describe in detail **two** ways in which *medical technology has improved the lifestyles of many elderly people.*

(Knowledge & Understanding, **4** marks)

(d)

"Single parent families and the long term unemployed receive financial help from the Government. Some MPs think *that the Government should provide less help and that individuals and families should do more to help* themselves."

Choose **either** single parent families **or** the long term unemployed.

What arguments could be put forward to **support** or **oppose** the view *that the Government should provide less help and that individuals and families should do more to help* the group you have chosen?

(Knowledge & Understanding, **4** marks)

SYLLABUS AREA 3—IDEOLOGIES

QUESTION 3

Answer **ONE** Section only: Section (A)—The USA on pages six and seven

                           OR Section (B)—Russia on pages eight and nine

                           OR Section (C)—China on pages ten and eleven

(A) THE USA

(a)

> "The capitalist system in the United States of America (USA) allows *many American citizens to have a high standard of living*."

In what ways does the capitalist **economic** system in the USA allow *many American citizens to have a high standard of living*?

(Knowledge & Understanding, **4** marks)

(b)

> "In the USA, African-Americans (Blacks) and Hispanic Americans are *less likely to achieve* **social** *and* **political** *success* than white Americans."

For what reasons are Black and Hispanic Americans *less likely to achieve* **social** and **political** *success* in the USA?

(Knowledge & Understanding, **6** marks)

(c)   Study Sources 1, 2 and 3 below and opposite, then answer the question which follows.

SOURCE 1

Immigration—an issue in the 1996 presidential election campaign

Bill Clinton's view	Bob Dole's view
President Clinton has taken steps to try and reduce illegal immigration. Border patrols have increased by 50%. Government contracts will not be given to firms employing illegal immigrants. He also wants a gradual reduction in legal immigration.	Senator Dole wishes to see even greater increases in border controls. He would like to make it easier and quicker to deport illegal immigrants back to the country from which they came. He supports the proposal in California to cut off public benefits from illegal immigrants.

Source: Adapted from *Time Magazine*, November 1996

QUESTION 3 (CONTINUED)

SOURCE 2

American citizens' attitudes to immigration

Opinion poll question

Do you believe that it should be made **easier** or **more difficult** for people from the following places to come to live in the United States?

Place of origin	Should be easier	Should be more difficult
China	32%	49%
Africa	31%	45%
Latin America	30%	47%
Eastern Europe	39%	39%

Source: Adapted from *Newsweek*, August 1993

SOURCE 3

Immigration and the economy

"Immigrants can bring economic advantages and disadvantages. When large numbers first enter a state it can put great pressure on health, welfare and education services which all require more public money. Recent figures show that the effect of all immigrants was to increase USA government spending by $50 billion in one year. However, the immigrants also paid $20 billion in taxes. In the early 1990s, 8% of native-born Californians received welfare compared with 10% of new immigrants. On average, Hispanic incomes are only 60% of the California average resulting in lower wage costs for firms that employ them. Some industries, such as agriculture, rely heavily on these workers, for example at harvest time."

Professor Kay Scott

View of an unemployed white American

American politicians are not concerned about immigration into the USA. A large majority of Americans think immigration should be made more difficult from all parts of the world. Immigration is having a damaging effect upon the American economy.

Using the information in Sources 1, 2, and 3 opposite and above, explain why the unemployed white American could be accused of being **selective** in the use of facts.

(Evaluating, **8** marks)

NOW GO TO QUESTION 4 ON PAGE THIRTEEN

QUESTION 3 (CONTINUED)

(B) RUSSIA

(a)

> "There have been many **political** changes in Russia since 1989."

Describe the **political** changes that have taken place in Russia since 1989.

(Knowledge & Understanding, **4** marks)

(b)

> "Many Russians believe that *they were better off under Communism*."

For what **social** and **economic** reasons do many Russians believe that *they were better off under Communism?*

(Knowledge & Understanding, **6** marks)

(c)   Study Sources 1, 2 and 3 below and opposite, then answer the question which follows.

SOURCE 1

Soldiers' views	
View of Chechen soldier	**View of Russian soldier**
Most Chechens are Moslems. We have always hated being ruled by Russians who do not share our religious beliefs. We have chosen our chief commander as President in free elections and want him to lead us to full independence. The war cost the Russians over $5 billion. Our army has proved superior. We were able to force the Russian army to leave Chechnya.	Chechnya has always been part of Russia and 35% of the population are Russian not Chechen. Russians and some Chechens want to stay as part of Russia. Our attempts to make peace were held up by unreasonable demands for Chechen independence. Over 120 Russian soldiers died after cease-fires were broken by the Chechen rebels. We agreed to withdraw from Chechnya to save lives.

QUESTION 3 (CONTINUED)

SOURCE 2

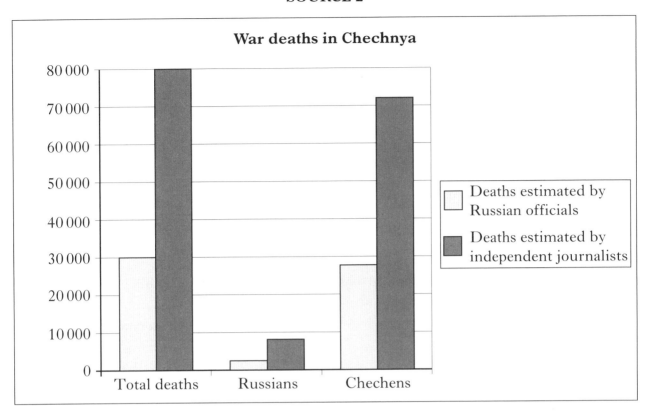

War deaths in Chechnya

SOURCE 3

Has peace come to Chechnya?

In 1996 Russia signed a cease-fire with Chechen forces. All Russian troops left Chechnya. In 1997 a peace treaty was signed by the Russian and Chechen Presidents. Both sides promised not to use force. However, violent incidents still occur in Chechnya as different groups disagree on how Chechnya should be run.

Elections were held in 1997 for a new regional government. Chechnya is to have more control of its own affairs. It is now called the Chechen Republic of Ishkezia, the name the rebels prefer.

The Chechen people will vote in a referendum to decide if Chechnya will have full independence. This could lead to civil war among Chechens. A final decision on Chechnya's status will be taken in 2001.

Source: Adapted from *The Economist*, September 1996 and the Centre for International Sociological Research, Moscow

View of a Russian politician

Everyone agrees that Chechnya should remain part of Russia because life in Chechnya is very similar to life in Russia. Casualties were light on all sides during the war which did very little damage. The war is now over and the recent peace agreement has solved all remaining problems.

Using Sources 1, 2 and 3 opposite and above, explain why the Russian politician could be accused of being **selective** in the use of facts.

(Evaluating, **8** marks)

NOW GO TO QUESTION 4 ON PAGE THIRTEEN

QUESTION 3 (CONTINUED)

(C) **CHINA**

(a)

> "The Communist Party *is the only political party allowed in China*."

Explain, in detail, why the Communist Party *is the only political party allowed in China*.

(Knowledge & Understanding, **4** marks)

(b)

> "There have been major **social** and **economic** changes in China in recent years. These have given China a stronger economy but also *led to increased inequality among the Chinese people*."

In what ways have recent **social** and **economic** changes in China *led to increased inequality among the Chinese people*?

(Knowledge & Understanding, **6** marks)

(c) Study Sources, 1, 2 and 3 below and opposite, then answer the question which follows.

SOURCE 1

China and Hong Kong

A social and economic comparison

	China	Hong Kong		China	Hong Kong
Population (millions)	1304	6	Unemployment	no figures but widespread	under 2%
% in countryside	70%	5%			
% literacy	80%	91%	Wealth per person (dollars)	390	21 753
Infant mortality (deaths per 1000 births)	50	5	Consumer goods per 1000 people		
			TVs	27	260
			cars	1	40
			telephones	9	504

QUESTION 3 (CONTINUED)

SOURCE 2

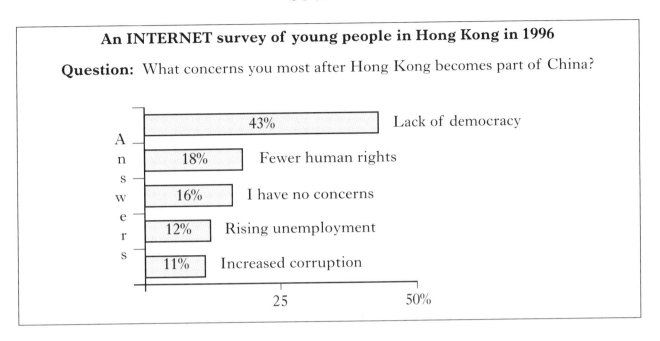

An INTERNET survey of young people in Hong Kong in 1996

Question: What concerns you most after Hong Kong becomes part of China?

- 43% — Lack of democracy
- 18% — Fewer human rights
- 16% — I have no concerns
- 12% — Rising unemployment
- 11% — Increased corruption

SOURCE 3

Hong Kong became a Special Administrative Region of China in 1997. The UK agreed that Hong Kong should become part of China provided that it could keep its way of life for at least 50 years. China describes this as One Country, Two Systems.

The free enterprise system that led Hong Kong to become a leading business and trading centre will continue. Over half of China's foreign trade comes through Hong Kong.

Hong Kong will have its own Government and law-making Council. The number of directly elected members of the Council will be increased. However, the Council elected in 1995 was abolished. China has refused to recognise Hong Kong's Bill of Rights. China's promises to respect human rights may not be kept. The Chinese army has moved into Hong Kong.

Sources: Foreign and Commonwealth Office and the Internet

View of a Chinese politician

Hong Kong and the rest of China are very similar. Everyone in Hong Kong is pleased that Hong Kong is part of China again. There have been no problems in Hong Kong's re-unification with China as the Chinese Government is not changing the way of life in Hong Kong.

Using Sources 1, 2 and 3 opposite and above, explain why the Chinese politician could be accused of being **selective** in the use of facts.

(Evaluating, **8** marks)

NOW GO TO QUESTION 4 ON PAGE THIRTEEN

[BLANK PAGE]

SYLLABUS AREA 4—INTERNATIONAL RELATIONS

QUESTION 4

(a)

> "Many East European countries now wish to join NATO and the European Union (EU). They believe there are many benefits."

Why do many East European countries want to join NATO and the European Union?

(Knowledge & Understanding, **8** marks)

[Turn over

QUESTION 4 (CONTINUED)

(b)   Study Sources 1, 2, 3 and 4 below and opposite on the European Union (EU) and answer the question which follows.

SOURCE 1

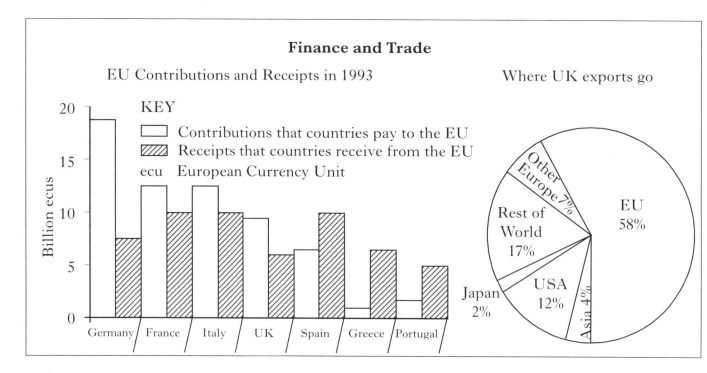

SOURCE 2

Agriculture and the EU Budget

The EU spends half of its Budget on agriculture. Farmers receive subsidies for much of the food they produce to make sure Europe is never short of food. Food that cannot be sold may have to be stored, sold at a loss, given away or even destroyed. On average UK farms are bigger and more efficient than the rest of the EU. Only 2% of UK workers are employed on farms which is well below the EU average of 5%. Over 10% of the workforce in Ireland, Spain, Portugal and Greece work in farming. The EU is now cutting back on subsidies and less unwanted food is being produced. Subsidies are now aimed at the poorest farmers, including Scottish crofters, and schemes to improve the countryside. However, agriculture will continue to be the most expensive part of the EU Budget.

SOURCE 3

Comparisons between the UK, EU and other major world economies in 1994

	UK	EU	USA	Japan
Average working week (hours)	37	35	35	39
Changes in earnings (1985 = 100)	109	114	91	123
Unemployment (%)	9·5	11·2	6·0	2·9
Increase in the cost of living (%)	2·5	3·1	2·6	0·7
GDP per person* (US dollars)	16 442	16 641	23 928	19 690

* GDP = Gross Domestic Product, a measure of the size of a country's economy

QUESTION 4 (CONTINUED)

SOURCE 4

Regions that qualify for financial assistance from the EU

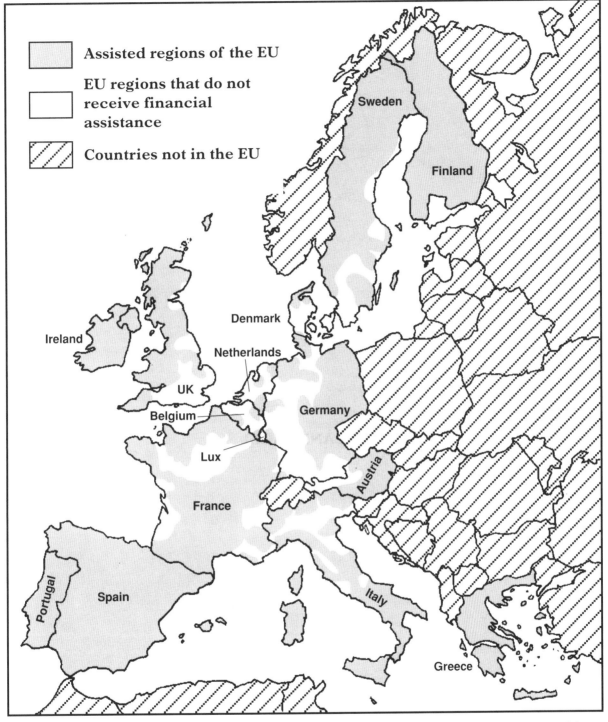

Sources: EUROSTAT and UN World Economic & Social Survey

> "The UK should leave the European Union."

Eurosceptic politician

Using Sources 1, 2, 3 and 4 opposite and above, say whether you **agree** or **disagree** with the view that the UK should leave the European Union.

You should give detailed reasons to **support** your choice **and** say why you rejected the other option.

(Evaluating, **10** marks)

[END OF QUESTION PAPER]

[BLANK PAGE]

2640/103

SCOTTISH
CERTIFICATE OF
EDUCATION
1999

WEDNESDAY, 19 MAY
10.50 AM – 12.50 PM

MODERN STUDIES
STANDARD GRADE
Credit Level

1 Read every question carefully.

2 Answer all questions as fully as you can.

3 If you cannot do a question, go on to the next one. Try again later.

4 In question 3, answer **one** section only.

5 Write your answers in the answer book provided. Indicate clearly, in the left hand margin, the question and section of question being answered. Do not write in the right hand margin.

SCOTTISH
QUALIFICATIONS
AUTHORITY

THB 2640/103 6/3/12520   ©

SYLLABUS AREA 1—LIVING IN A DEMOCRACY

QUESTION 1

(a) "Most UK citizens only **participate** in politics when they vote. However, there are many other ways in which they can **participate** in politics."

Apart from voting, in what ways can UK citizens **participate** in politics?

(Knowledge & Understanding, **8** marks)

(b) Study the Source below, then answer the question which follows.

What UK voters think MPs should be allowed to do (%):	Yes	No	No strong opinion
* Continue with a trade or profession (eg farmer, lawyer, dentist etc) as well as being an MP	45	33	22
* Be paid to write articles for newspapers	35	43	22
* Be paid to represent a pressure group	21	44	35
* Be sponsored by trade unions	21	48	31
* Receive fees for lobbying	3	78	19
* Ask parliamentary questions for money	8	83	9

Sources: Adapted from *British Politics*, David Roberts (ed), 1995

"A clear majority of UK voters think that their MPs should be full-time representatives with no outside interests."

Helen Page

For what reasons could Helen Page be accused of being **selective in her use of facts**?

Your reasons must be based entirely on the Source above.

(Enquiry Skills, **4** marks)

QUESTION 1 (CONTINUED)

(c)   Study the Source below, then answer the question which follows.

The % of UK employees who are members of Trade Unions

	All	Men	Women
All employees	31	33	29
Age group			
Under 20	6	6	6
20–29	23	23	24
30–39	34	35	33
40+	38	42	34
Ethnic origin			
White	31	33	29
Non-white	29	28	31
of which			
Black	36	33	39
Indian	29	30	28
Pakistani/ Bangla Deshi	17	15	21

Sources: Adapted from *Labour Market Trends*, June 1997

What **conclusions** can be reached about the extent to which UK employees participate in Trade Unions?

Your conclusions must be based entirely on the Source above.

(Enquiry Skills, **6** marks)

[Turn over

SYLLABUS AREA 2—CHANGING SOCIETY

QUESTION 2

(a)

> "*New technology* has *led to greater job opportunities for some workers than for others.*"

For what reasons has *new technology led to greater job opportunities for some workers than for others*?

(Knowledge and Understanding, **6** marks)

(b)

> Some politicians argue in favour of a **National Minimum Wage** while others argue against it.

Give **one** argument **for** and **one** argument **against** a **National Minimum Wage**.

(Knowledge and Understanding, **4** marks)

(c)   You have been asked to carry out an **investigation** into the problems faced by single parents in finding a suitable job.

(i)   State a relevant **hypothesis** for your investigation.

(Enquiry Skills, **2** marks)

(ii)   Give **two** aims or headings to help you prove or disprove your hypothesis.

(Enquiry Skills, **2** marks)

Choose **one** of the following **methods of enquiry** for your investigation:

the Internet, **or**
an interview with a single parent.

(iii)   For **one** of your aims, describe in detail how you would find information using your chosen method of enquiry.

(Enquiry Skills, **2** marks)

(iv)   Give **advantages** and **disadvantages** of your chosen method of enquiry as a source of information for this investigation.

(Enquiry Skills, **4** marks)

SYLLABUS AREA 3—IDEOLOGIES

QUESTION 3

Answer **ONE** Section only: Section (A)—The USA on pages five, six and seven

OR Section (B)—Russia on pages eight and nine

OR Section (C)—China on pages ten, eleven and twelve

(A) THE USA

(a)

> "In the USA, citizens have a number of **political rights**."

Describe, in detail, the **political rights** of American citizens.

(Knowledge & Understanding, **6** marks)

(b)   Study the Source below, then answer the question which follows.

Housing for Whites and Hispanics in the United States of America

Central City Areas	Whites	Hispanics
Percentage who own their own home	56%	33%
Average value of house	$76 200	$66 300
Houses with more than 1 person per room	2%	29%
Suburban Areas	**Whites**	**Hispanics**
Percentage who own their own home	74%	51%
Average value of house	$107 100	$99 200
Houses with more than 1 person per room	2%	27%

Source: US Department of Commerce, Bureau of the Census, March 1995

Using **only** the Source above, what **conclusions** can be reached about housing for Hispanic Americans compared with White Americans?

(Enquiry Skills, **4** marks)

[Turn over

QUESTION 3(A) (CONTINUED)

(c)   Study Sources 1, 2 and 3 below and opposite, then answer the question which follows.

SOURCE 1

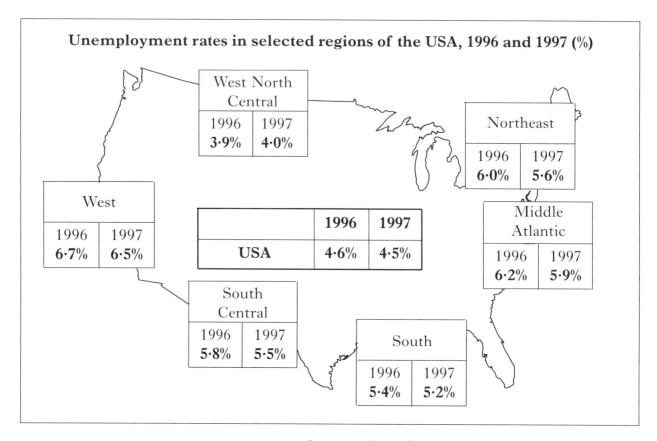

Source: Adapted from *US Bureau of Labor Statistics*, 1997

SOURCE 2

Extract from Report on US Economy by the International Monetary Fund (IMF)

Economic growth in the United States rose from 1·6% in 1995 to 4·9% in 1997. The unemployment rate was over 5% in 1995 and fell to below 5% by July 1997. The rise in the cost of living has fallen from 3% during 1995 to around 2·5% in 1997. There has been a reduction in the US Government's borrowing from $290 billion in 1992 to $107 billion in 1996. The value of the US dollar has increased by about 5%.

The IMF has warned the US government that the increased numbers of old people will place strains on the Social Security system. The IMF is also concerned that the high level of demand for goods and services and low unemployment could lead to economic problems in the future.

Source: Adapted from *International Monetary Fund Press Notice*, August 1997

QUESTION 3(A) (CONTINUED)

SOURCE 3

Answers to Opinion Poll of US Citizens

Do you worry about losing your job?

Is the USA going through a period of good times or bad times right now?

	Total	Men	Women
Good times	54%	59%	49%
Bad times	33%	25%	39%
Some Good, some Bad	12%	15%	9%

Bar chart: Yes — 1996: 31%, 1997: 20%. No — 1996: 69%, 1997: 80%.

Legend: 1996, 1997

Source: Adapted from *Time Magazine*, May 1997

View of a Republican politician

"Recent US Government policies have damaged the American economy."

Using **only** the Sources above and opposite, explain why the Republican politician could be accused of being **selective** in the use of facts.

Your answer must be based entirely on Sources 1, 2 and 3 above and opposite.

(Enquiry Skills, **8** marks)

NOW GO TO QUESTION 4 ON PAGE THIRTEEN

QUESTION 3 (CONTINUED)

(B) **RUSSIA**

(a) Study Sources 1, 2 and 3 below, then answer the question which follows.

SOURCE 1

Russian economic indicators				
	1993	*1994*	*1995*	*1996*
Economic Growth/Decline (+/−%)	−8	−12·6	−4	+3
Unemployment (%)	5·5	7·1	8·3	9·3
Days lost in strikes (thousands)	237	755	1367	4009
Yearly increase in prices (%)	840	215	131	22

SOURCE 2

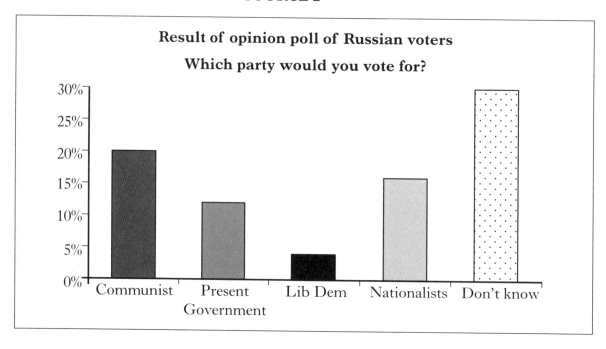

Result of opinion poll of Russian voters

Which party would you vote for?

SOURCE 3

Living conditions in Russia today
Foreign companies like McDonald's pay much better wages than people earned under Communism. However, most ordinary Russians feel worse off as unemployment has risen and 25% of the people now live below the official poverty line. Diseases like TB are becoming more common and average life expectancy has fallen from 63 years to 58 years. Crime has increased with increasing violence and robbery on the streets. The government finds it difficult to collect taxes due to corruption. Some Russians have been able to build expensive houses, but ordinary Russians cannot afford a new home as the Government cannot afford to build houses.

Source: Adapted from *Russian Economic Trends*, December 1997 from the Internet

QUESTION 3(B) (CONTINUED)

> "The Government has the support of the people because the economy and living conditions have improved."

Spokesperson for the Russian Government

Using **only** the Sources opposite, explain why the spokesperson for the Russian Government could be accused of being **selective** in the use of facts.

Your answer must be based entirely on Sources 1, 2 and 3 opposite.

(Enquiry Skills, **8** marks)

(b)

> "In Russia, citizens now have many **political rights**."

Describe, in detail, the **political rights** of Russian citizens.

(Knowledge and Understanding, **6** marks)

(c) Study the Source below, then answer the question which follows.

Selected Towns in Russia

St.Petersburg	Moscow	Sverdlovsk
Economic Growth 2·9%	Economic Growth 6·3%	Economic Growth 5·9%
Households with phone 39%	Households with phone 50%	Households with phone 19%
Income per head $2155	Income per head $6127	Income per head $1599

RUSSIA

Nizhny Novgorod	Irkutsk
Economic Growth 4%	Economic Growth 4·1%
Households with phone 18%	Households with phone 11%
Income per head $1211	Income per head $1915

What **conclusions** can be reached about differences in living standards between residents of selected towns in Russia today?

Your answer must be based entirely on the Source above.

(Enquiry Skills, **4** marks)

NOW GO TO QUESTION 4 ON PAGE THIRTEEN

QUESTION 3 (CONTINUED)

(C) **CHINA**

(*a*) Study Sources 1, 2, and 3 below and opposite, then answer the question which follows.

SOURCE 1

Percentage of households in different income groups in China (US dollars)

	1985	1990	1995	2000 [estimate]
$0 – $3,000	99·6%	98·7%	90·1%	88·0%
$3,001 – $6,000	0·4%	1·3%	9·3%	10·8%
$6,001 – $9,000	0·0%	0·0%	0·6%	1·2%

SOURCE 2

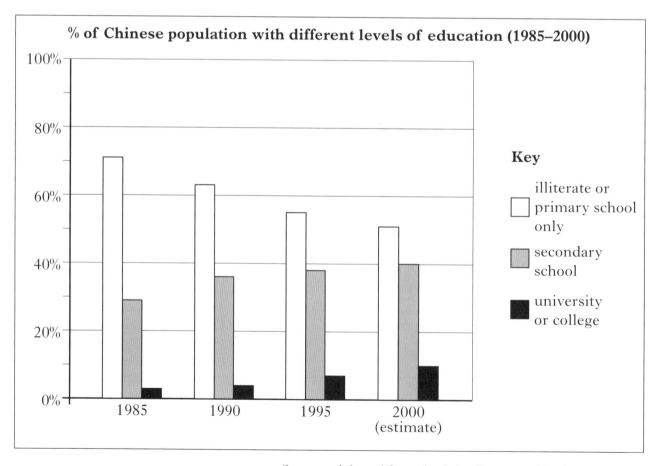

Sources: Adapted from the Asian Demographics Internet Site

QUESTION 3(C) (CONTINUED)

SOURCE 3

Deng Xiaoping, the Chinese leader, died in February 1997. Many of the reforms he introduced left the people of China worse off. Most state owned industries make a loss because they employ too many people and produce too little. Most of them will be sold off and so lead to widespread unemployment. Crime and violence continue to increase. Since Deng's death, the government has introduced a plan which aims to eliminate poverty. Improved living standards and better medical care will help Chinese people live longer. Infant mortality was 250 per 1000 births in 1950 but today it is only 37 per 1000 births. The government will also increase the number of Special Economic Zones, areas where more reform is planned.

Political expert on Asia

Source: Adapted from *The Scotsman*, February 1997

View of a Chinese peasant farmer

"The reforms in China introduced by Deng Xiaoping have not worked."

Explain why the Chinese peasant farmer could be accused of being **selective in the use of facts**.

Your answer must be based entirely on Sources 1, 2 and 3 above and opposite.

(Enquiry Skills, **8** marks)

[Turn over

QUESTION 3 (C) (CONTINUED)

(b)

> In China the government limits *the **political rights*** *of Chinese citizens.*

In what ways does the government limit *the **political rights*** *of Chinese citizens?*

(Knowledge & Understanding, **6** marks)

(c)   Study the Source below, then answer the question which follows.

Statistics on different regions in China

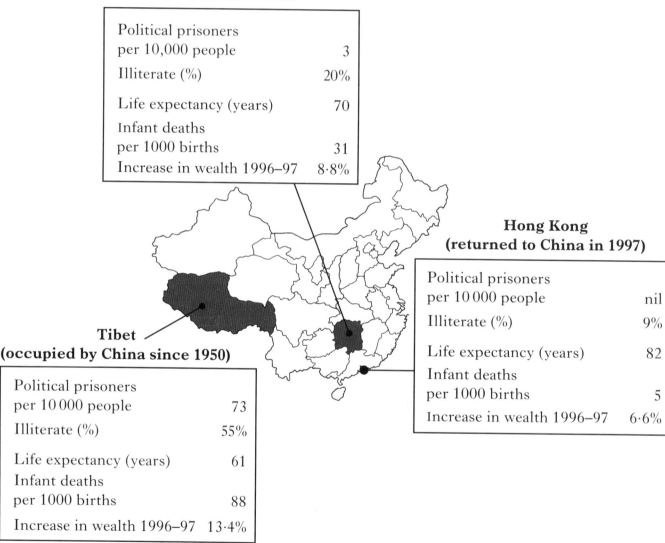

Hunan Province

Political prisoners per 10,000 people	3
Illiterate (%)	20%
Life expectancy (years)	70
Infant deaths per 1000 births	31
Increase in wealth 1996–97	8·8%

Hong Kong (returned to China in 1997)

Political prisoners per 10 000 people	nil
Illiterate (%)	9%
Life expectancy (years)	82
Infant deaths per 1000 births	5
Increase in wealth 1996–97	6·6%

Tibet (occupied by China since 1950)

Political prisoners per 10 000 people	73
Illiterate (%)	55%
Life expectancy (years)	61
Infant deaths per 1000 births	88
Increase in wealth 1996–97	13·4%

Source: *The New Internationalist*, December 1995 and the Internet

What **conclusions** can be reached about regional differences in China?

Your answer must be based entirely on the Source above.

(Enquiry Skills, **4** marks)

NOW GO TO QUESTION 4 ON PAGE THIRTEEN

SYLLABUS AREA 4—INTERNATIONAL RELATIONS

QUESTION 4

(*a*)

> "The media often show African countries receiving emergency aid after a disaster. However, long term development aid can be more important in meeting the *needs of African countries*."

Describe ways in which aid can meet the *needs of African countries* you have studied.

(Knowledge & Understanding, **8** marks)

[Turn over

QUESTION 4 (CONTINUED)

(b) Study Sources 1, 2, 3 and 4 below and opposite, then answer the question which follows.

SOURCE 1

Recent political changes in Africa

Many African countries were ruled by dictators who often used military force. Since 1989, many African countries have held multi-party elections, although in some of them corruption and threats were used. By 1997, twelve countries had become democracies with a choice of political parties. These include South Africa, where everyone, black and white, can vote now apartheid has ended. Other countries, such as Ethiopia and Uganda, are limited democracies. They have elections but opposition parties are discouraged. Fewer countries, such as Sudan, are ruled by one tribal or religious group which does not allow others equal rights. In some countries, such as Congo-Zaire, one dictator has been replaced by another. Civil war still affects many parts of Africa, such as Rwanda, where recently over a million people were killed.

SOURCE 2

Economic indicators for four of the largest countries in Africa

	Wealth per person US $		Total external debt in US $ (millions)		% average annual economic growth
Year	1982	1993	1982	1992	1985–93
Ethiopia	140	100	875	4400	+1·8
Nigeria	860	310	6085	31 015	+3·2
South Africa	2670	2900	not available	16 600	−1·5
Congo-Zaire	190	250	4087	10 300	−6·0

Source: Adapted from World Development Report, Geographical Digest

SOURCE 3

Social indicators for four of the largest countries in Africa

	Calories per person per day (recommended intake is 2500 cal)		Infant mortality per 1000 births		% wealth spent on education	
Year	1980	1992	1982	1995	1988	1990
Ethiopia	1858	1610	122	119	4·1	4·5
Nigeria	2246	2124	109	96	2·2	1·0
South Africa	2932	2635	55	62	3·8	6·4
Congo-Zaire	2126	2062	106	75	5·8	1·0

Source: Adapted from UNESCO Statistics Yearbook and the World Statistics Pocket Book

QUESTION 4 (CONTINUED)

SOURCE 4

African countries and trade

Deficit: more imports than exports in 1993

Surplus: more exports than imports in 1993

One in three African people live in the four countries named on the map.

Sources: Adapted from UN Statistics published in a Third World Guide, the MSA Yearbook and Understanding Global Issues

Newspaper Editorial

Countries in Africa have not made political, social or economic progress in recent years.

Using **only** the Sources above and opposite, provide evidence **for** and **against** the view of the newspaper editorial.

Your answer must be based entirely on Sources 1, 2, 3 and 4 above and opposite.

Overall, do you think the evidence supports the view?

(Enquiry Skills, **10** marks)

[END OF QUESTION PAPER]

[BLANK PAGE]

2640/403

NATIONAL
QUALIFICATIONS
2000

THURSDAY, 8 JUNE
10.50 AM – 12.50 PM

MODERN STUDIES
STANDARD GRADE
Credit Level

1   Read every question carefully.

2   Answer all questions as fully as you can.

3   If you cannot do a question, go on to the next one. Try again later.

4   In question 3, answer **one** section only.

5   Write your answers in the answer book provided. Indicate clearly, in the left hand margin, the question and section of question being answered. Do not write in the right hand margin.

SCOTTISH
QUALIFICATIONS
AUTHORITY
©

SYLLABUS AREA 1—LIVING IN A DEMOCRACY

QUESTION 1

(a) | "Elections to the UK parliament at Westminster use the *First Past The Post System*. Elections to the Scottish Parliament use the *Additional Member System*."

Choose **either** the *First Past the Post System* **or** the *Additional Member System*. Explain the **advantages** of the system you have chosen.

(Knowledge & Understanding, **6** marks)

(b) | "The turnout at UK elections is seldom over 70%. *People should use their vote.*"

Why is it important that *people should use their vote?*

(Knowledge & Understanding, **4** marks)

QUESTION 1 (CONTINUED)

You have been asked to carry out an investigation on the topic below.

Investigation Topic—The methods used by pressure groups to influence MPs.

Now answer questions (c), (d), (e) and (f) which follow.

(c)   State a relevant **hypothesis** for your investigation.

(Enquiry Skills, **2** marks)

(d)   Give **two** aims or headings to help you prove **or** disprove your hypothesis.

(Enquiry Skills, **2** marks)

(e)   You decide to visit a library to help with your investigation.

For **one** of your chosen aims or headings, describe how you would find information using a library.

(Enquiry Skills, **2** marks)

(f)   You also decide to use a questionnaire.

Describe, **in detail**, **two** possible **disadvantages** of a questionnaire as a method of finding out information for this investigation.

(Enquiry Skills, **4** marks)

[Turn over

SYLLABUS AREA 2—CHANGING SOCIETY

QUESTION 2

(a) | "Residential care is the best way of meeting the needs of some elderly people." |

Explain, **in detail**, why *residential care is the best way of meeting the needs of some elderly people.*

(Knowledge and Understanding, **6** marks)

(b) Study Sources 1, 2 and 3 below and opposite, then answer the question which follows.

SOURCE 1

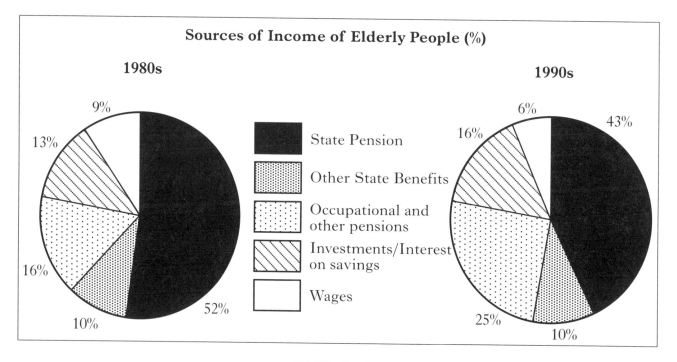

Sources of Income of Elderly People (%)

1980s — 9%, 13%, 16%, 10%, 52%

1990s — 6%, 16%, 43%, 25%, 10%

Legend:
- State Pension
- Other State Benefits
- Occupational and other pensions
- Investments/Interest on savings
- Wages

SOURCE 2

Living on a Pension

For married couples, the average state pension provides £109·35 compared to the average earnings of £336·80 per week. Although the income of older people has improved in recent years, the poverty rate among older people is still high. The two main reasons are age and gender.

Recently retired people now have greater access to newer forms of private pensions whereas older retired people still rely mostly on state pensions, benefits or assistance from their families.

Inequalities also exist between older women and men. Women are likely to retire with less income than men, but are more likely to live into very old age.

Recently, the average income of pensioners has risen by about 70% more than the rate of inflation, but averages hide huge inequalities. Since the early 1980s, the richest single pensioners have increased their income by 81% (£81) but for the poorest, the increase was only 28% (£12).

Source: Adapted from Age Concern data

QUESTION 2 (CONTINUED)

SOURCE 3

Survey on Financial Situation of Elderly in European Union (%)				
	UK	**Denmark**	**Greece**	**Netherlands**
Very Poor	4	2	15	2
Poor	9	3	35	6
Reasonably well-off	43	20	32	39
Very well-off	44	75	18	53

Source: Adapted from Centre for Policy on Ageing

"There has been very little change in the source of income received by pensioners in recent years. The income of pensioners, regardless of age or gender, is very low. Older pensioners are just as likely to have a good pension as those who are in their sixties. In spite of their difficulties, most elderly people in the UK manage to meet their needs easily, unlike those in other European Union countries."

View of Adam Young

Using Sources 1, 2 and 3 above and opposite, explain why Adam Young could be accused of being **selective in the use of facts**.

Your reasons must be based entirely on Sources 1, 2, and 3.

(Enquiry Skills, **8** marks)

(c) *"Lone parents may have more difficulty in finding suitable employment than other groups."*

Explain, **in detail**, why *lone parents may have more difficulty in finding suitable employment than other groups*.

(Knowledge and Understanding, **4** marks)

[Turn over

SYLLABUS AREA 3—IDEOLOGIES

QUESTION 3

Answer **ONE** Section only: Section (A)—The USA on pages six, seven and eight

                                 OR Section (B)—Russia on pages nine, ten, eleven and twelve

                                 OR Section (C)—China on pages thirteen, fourteen and fifteen

(A) **THE USA**

(a)   Study Sources 1, 2, 3 and 4 below and opposite, then answer the question which follows.

SOURCE 1

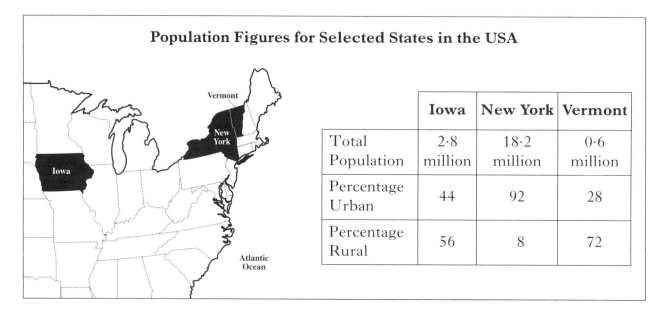

Population Figures for Selected States in the USA

	Iowa	New York	Vermont
Total Population	2·8 million	18·2 million	0·6 million
Percentage Urban	44	92	28
Percentage Rural	56	8	72

SOURCE 2

Crime in Selected States

	Iowa	New York	Vermont
Violent crimes per 100 000 population	273	727	121
Prisoners per 100 000 population	223	384	191

QUESTION 3(A) (CONTINUED)

SOURCE 3

Income and Poverty in Selected States

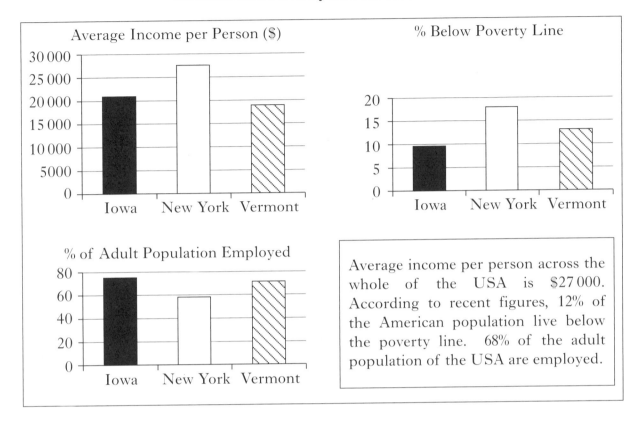

SOURCE 4

Health Issues in Selected States

	Iowa	New York	Vermont
Percentage of population with no health insurance	12·0%	17·5%	9·5%
Doctors per 100 000 people	169·0	366·0	277·0
Infant deaths per 1000 births	7·9	8·1	6·0
Percentage of births to mothers aged under 20	11·0%	9·0%	9·2%

Use only the information in Sources 1, 2, 3 and 4 above and opposite. Compare the information on the 3 selected states. What **conclusions** can be drawn about Population, Crime, Income and Poverty and Health Care in these selected states of the USA?

(Enquiry Skills, **8** marks)

[Turn over

QUESTION 3(A) (CONTINUED)

(b)   Study Sources 1 and 2 below, then answer the question which follows.

SOURCE 1

Profile of the 106th Congress of the USA				
Group	% House of Representatives	% Senate	% Total	% US Population
White	86·6	97·0	88·6	71·0
Black	8·6	0·0	6·9	13·0
Hispanic	4·1	0·0	3·4	11·0
Asian/Pacific Islander	0·7	2·0	0·9	4·0
Native American	0·0	1·0	0·2	1·0

SOURCE 2

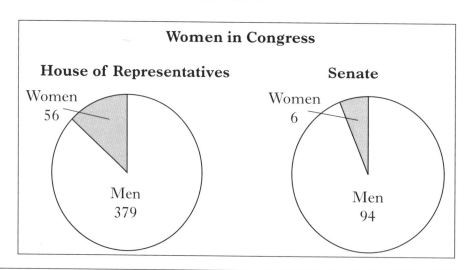

"All groups in the USA are fairly represented in Congress."

View of Donna Kennedy

Using only the information in Sources 1 and 2 above, explain why Donna Kennedy could be accused of being **selective in the use of facts**.

(Enquiry Skills, **4** marks)

(c)   *"The rights of American people are protected by the Constitution."*

Describe, **in detail**, how *the rights of American people are protected by the Constitution.*

(Knowledge and Understanding, **4** marks)

NOW GO TO QUESTION 4 ON PAGE SEVENTEEN

QUESTION 3 (CONTINUED)

(B) **RUSSIA**

(a)   Study Sources 1 and 2 below, then answer the question that follows.

SOURCE 1

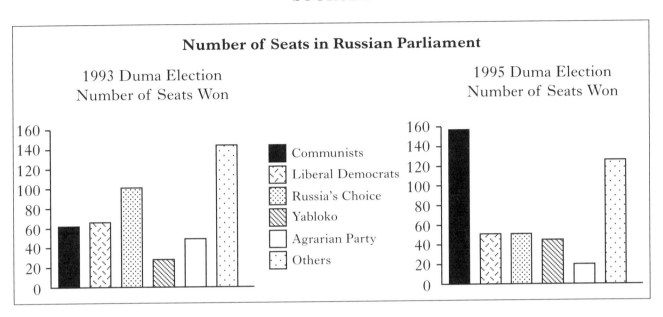

Number of Seats in Russian Parliament

1993 Duma Election
Number of Seats Won

1995 Duma Election
Number of Seats Won

■ Communists
⊠ Liberal Democrats
▨ Russia's Choice
▧ Yabloko
□ Agrarian Party
⋯ Others

SOURCE 2

Russian Presidential Election—1996 (First Ballot)		
Candidate	*Party*	*Percentage of Votes*
Vladimir Bryantslov	Independent	0·2
Svyatoslav Fyodorov	Party of Worker's Self-Rule	0·9
Mikhail Gorbachev	Independent	0·5
Alexander Lebed	Congress of Russian Communities	14·5
Martin Shakkum	Independent	0·4
Yuri Vlasov	Russia's Choice	0·2
Grigory Yavlinsky	Yabloko	7·3
Boris Yeltsin	Independent	35·3
Vladimir Zhirinovsky	Liberal Democrats	5·7
Gennady Zyuganov	Communist	32·0
Spoiled Papers		3·0

"The Russian people have a clear opinion about which Party should control the Duma and provide the President."

View of Russian Journalist

Using **only** Sources 1 and 2 above, explain why the Russian journalist could be accused of being **selective in the use of facts**.

(Enquiry Skills, **4** marks)

QUESTION 3(B) (CONTINUED)

(b)   Study Sources 1, 2, 3 and 4 below and opposite, then answer the question which follows.

SOURCE 1

RUSSIAN DAILY NEWS

May 26 1999   For All The Best News   40k

REGIONAL LEADERS SPEAK OUT

Politicians in Russia's remoter regions have spoken out about the economic crisis facing their areas.

A spokesperson for the Government in Moscow said that all parts of Russia were treated equally. "We hand out generous subsidies to help the economy in all parts of Russia. No area should feel that it is being treated any better or worse than any other part of Russia," he said.

"Although Russia as a whole is attracting foreign investment, most of the benefits are only being seen in Moscow and far west of the country.

Here in Krasnoyarsk, in the east of Russia, we do not benefit," said Ludmila Yuranov, representative of the Krasnoyarsk Regional Government.

"The Government in Moscow does not give us a fair deal. We send tax revenues to Moscow and in return they send us subsidies. Last year we sent far more in tax revenues than they gave us in subsidies. This is already a poor region and it is becoming poorer. In Russia today the rich are getting richer and the poor are getting poorer," she continued.

QUESTION 3(B) (CONTINUED)

SOURCE 2

Wages in Russia

NOTICE TO WORKERS

The factory management regret that we are again unable to pay your wages this week, due to the economic crisis. We intend to pay you everything you are due as soon as possible.

S. Noltsin (Manager)

Wage Arrears in Russia by Region:

Region	Percentage of Workers:	
	Paid in full and on time	*Paid in part and late*
Moscow	76·8	5·4
Krasnoyarsk	34·7	22·1
Chuvash Republic	42·5	14·2
Chelyabinsk	33·7	23·5

SOURCE 3

Type of Employment—New Jobs available in Selected Areas of Russia (%)

Area	Permanent	Fixed Term	Casual
Moscow	84	12	4
Krasnoyarsk	87	12	1
Chuvash Republic	92	7	1
Chelyabinsk	93	5	2

Fixed-term and casual jobs do not provide job security. People cannot make long-term plans because they do not know what their income will be in the future. Permanent employment is the best way to improve living standards.

View of a Russian Economist

SOURCE 4

Regional Results in the 1996 Russian Presidential Elections
(Percentage of the Vote)

Region \ Candidate	Yeltsin (Independent)	Zyuganov (Communist)	Lebed (Congress)	Zhirinovsky (Liberal Democrat)	Yavlinsky (Yabloko)
Moscow	61·7	15·0	9·7	1·5	8·0
Krasnoyarsk	35·3	28·9	14·1	7·7	10·1
Chuvash Republic	21·3	56·0	8·0	4·4	4·8
Chelyabinsk	37·2	25·1	20·2	5·3	8·9

Using **only** the information in Sources 1, 2, 3 and 4 above and opposite, compare the information about economic conditions and political opinion in different parts of Russia. What **conclusions** can be drawn about the differences in both economic inequality and political opinion in the various parts of Russia?

(Enquiry Skills, **8** marks)

QUESTION 3(B) (CONTINUED)

(c) | *"The human rights of Russian people have improved in recent years."* |

Describe, **in detail**, how *the human rights of Russian people have improved in recent years*.

(Knowledge and Understanding, **4** marks)

NOW GO TO QUESTION 4 ON PAGE SEVENTEEN

QUESTION 3 (CONTINUED)

(C) **CHINA**

(a) | *"The human rights of Chinese people have changed in recent years."* |
     |---|

Describe, **in detail**, how *the Human Rights of the Chinese people have changed in recent years.*

(Knowledge and Understanding, **4** marks)

(b) Study Sources 1 and 2 below, then answer the question which follows.

SOURCE 1

Background of Members of the National People's Congress (1993–1998)

Background of Deputy	Percent
Cadres	28·0
Intellectuals	22·0
Other Party Workers	19·0
Ordinary Workers	11·0
Farmers	9·5
Army	9·0
Returned Overseas Chinese	1·5

Male/Female Members of the National People's Congress

21% Female
79% Male

The 55 national minorities are represented by 15% of the deputies.

SOURCE 2

Political Parties in China

Party	Membership
Communist Party	57 000 000
China Democratic League	105 000
China Democratic National Construction Association	50 000
China Association for Promoting Democracy	50 000
China Revolutionary Committee of the Kuomingtang	40 000
China Peasants and Workers Democratic Party	40 000
Jiusan Society	40 000
Chinese Party for Public Interest	10 000

"People are wrong to criticise the Chinese political system. The eighth National People's Congress is very democratic because ordinary workers and farmers make up the majority of the deputies. The Communist Party may be the biggest, but there are many other strong parties that people can vote for."

Statement by Ye Zhen

Using **only** Sources 1 and 2 above, explain why Ye Zhen could be accused of being **selective in the use of facts**.

(Enquiry Skills, **4** marks)

QUESTION 3(C) (CONTINUED)

(c)   Study Sources 1, 2, 3 and 4 below and opposite, then answer the question which follows.

SOURCE 1

Population and GDP in Selected Regions of China		
Region	Percentage of China's population	Percentage of China's GDP (Wealth)
Beijing	0·90	2·38
Guangdong	5·39	9·62
Shanghai	1·00	4·28
Sichaun	9·00	6·22

SOURCE 2

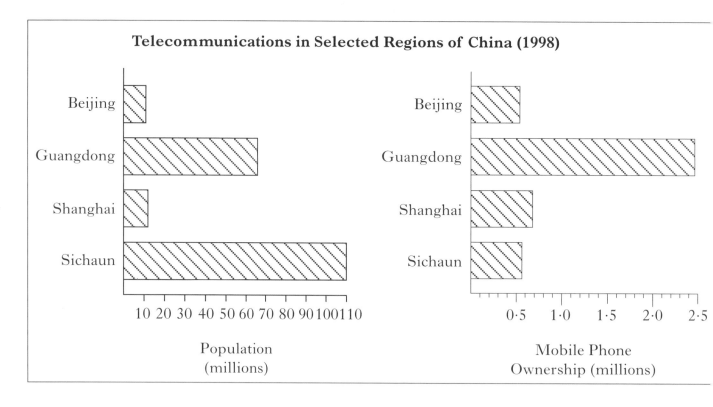

Telecommunications in Selected Regions of China (1998)

QUESTION 3(C) (CONTINUED)

SOURCE 3

China—Level of Access to Public Utilities in Cities in Selected Regions

Region	Percentage of population with tap water	Percentage of population with gas supply	Number of public toilets per 10 000 people
Beijing	100·0	92·7	11·2
Guangdong	95·2	90·0	2·7
Shanghai	100·0	91·4	1·3
Sichuan	95·3	66·1	5·0
National Average	94·9	73·2	5·8

SOURCE 4

The Economic Revolution in China

Over the last fifteen years China has undergone an economic revolution. Greater links with Europe and the United States have opened up new markets in China, and multi-national companies have been quick to move in. Chinese businesses have also been allowed to grow as the Government lessens its control over the economy.

The results have been spectacular. In regions such as Guangdong and Shanghai the living standards for many people have improved very quickly. They now enjoy the sort of lifestyles that people in Europe and the USA have had for years. Most Chinese people hope that economic progress and development will continue. Some are frightened that NATO's bombing raid on the Chinese Embassy in Belgrade will upset relations between China and the West and that relations could suffer because of that.

Not everyone in China has seen the benefits of the economic revolution. In rural areas and in remote provinces such as Sichaun, economic progress has been slow.

Using **only** Sources 1, 2, 3 and 4 above and opposite, compare the information about different regions in China. What **conclusions** can be drawn about regional inequalities in China?

(Enquiry Skills, **8** marks)

NOW GO TO QUESTION 4 ON PAGE SEVENTEEN

[BLANK PAGE]

SYLLABUS AREA 4—INTERNATIONAL RELATIONS

QUESTION 4

(a)

> "Membership of the European Union has grown to 15 countries. More countries are keen to join the EU."

Explain, **in detail**, the main arguments **for** and **against** expanding the membership of the European Union.

(Knowledge & Understanding, **8** marks)

[Turn over

QUESTION 4 (CONTINUED)

(b)   Study Sources 1, 2, 3 and 4 below and opposite, then answer the questions which follow.

SOURCE 1

Selected European Security Flashpoints

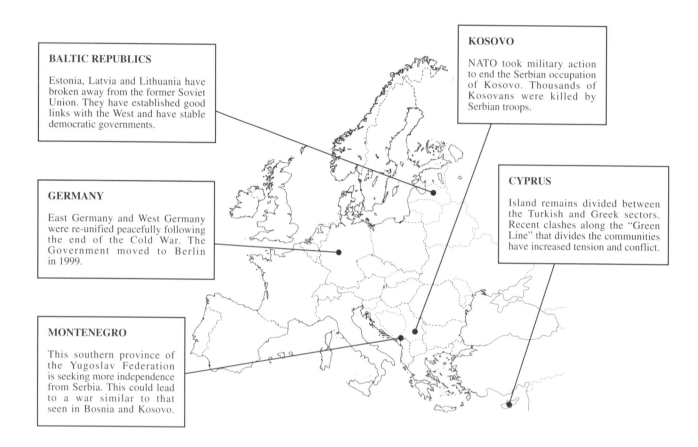

BALTIC REPUBLICS

Estonia, Latvia and Lithuania have broken away from the former Soviet Union. They have established good links with the West and have stable democratic governments.

GERMANY

East Germany and West Germany were re-unified peacefully following the end of the Cold War. The Government moved to Berlin in 1999.

MONTENEGRO

This southern province of the Yugoslav Federation is seeking more independence from Serbia. This could lead to a war similar to that seen in Bosnia and Kosovo.

KOSOVO

NATO took military action to end the Serbian occupation of Kosovo. Thousands of Kosovans were killed by Serbian troops.

CYPRUS

Island remains divided between the Turkish and Greek sectors. Recent clashes along the "Green Line" that divides the communities have increased tension and conflict.

SOURCE 2

NEW YORK COURIER

May 23 2000   50c

CLOSURE OF MILITARY BASES CAUSES ECONOMIC CHANGES

The full effect of the "Peace Dividend" is only now being felt in Europe, particularly in Germany. Several large American military bases have been closed. It is estimated that more than 10 000 German civilian workers have lost their jobs.

Britain has also cut back the strength of its forces in Germany. Businesses that used to supply the military with weapons systems and other equipment have been badly hit—some have had to close down.

Unless there is an increase in military spending, many more places will suffer through job losses and business closures.

QUESTION 4 (CONTINUED)

SOURCE 3

Views of a University Professor and a Leading Politician

STATEMENT FROM UNIVERSITY PROFESSOR

One of the most serious problems affecting Europe today is Nationalism. For example, in Turkey the Kurdish separatists have launched many terrorist attacks against ordinary people, including British tourists. Yugoslavia has been torn apart, with thousands of people killed in the fighting in Croatia, Bosnia and Kosovo. Nationalist feelings are strong throughout Europe and NATO must be ready to respond by having a Task Force.

STATEMENT FROM LEADING POLITICIAN

Military power solves nothing. The way to solve problems is through diplomacy and negotiation. Czechoslovakia split into two in a peaceful way. In the recent wars in Yugoslavia it was not military force that brought about peace settlements—it was negotiations and meetings behind the scenes. Europe needs more political and diplomatic contact, not more weapons and troops.

SOURCE 4

Operation Allied Force—The NATO Campaign against Serbia

NATO PLANE SHOT DOWN OVER SERBIA

BRITISH SOLDIERS KILLED DEFUSING LANDMINES

AMERICAN SOLDIERS TAKEN PRISONER BY SERBS

THE FINANCIAL COST

The cost of the NATO bombing campaign has been estimated at £4800 million. Britain's contribution is about 12 per cent. Britain will pay 14 per cent of the European Union's (EU's) expenditure on rebuilding Kosovo.

THE HUMAN COST

It is believed that there were substantial numbers of military casualties in Yugoslavia. There were also civilian casualties, though that was not NATO's intention.

"NATO is considering establishing a Rapid Reaction Task Force which would be made up of highly-trained soldiers from various NATO countries. It would be based in Europe and would be able to be transported rapidly to any area to prevent conflict."

(i) Using information from Sources 1, 2, 3 and 4 above and opposite, give arguments **for** and **against** the proposal to set up a Rapid Reaction Task Force.

(Enquiry Skills, **8** marks)

(ii) Overall, do you support the proposal? **Explain** why you have reached this decision. You should only use information from the sources in your answer.

(Enquiry Skills, **2** marks)

[END OF QUESTION PAPER]

[BLANK PAGE]

2640/403

NATIONAL
QUALIFICATIONS
2001

FRIDAY, 1 JUNE
10.50 AM – 12.50 PM

MODERN STUDIES
STANDARD GRADE
Credit Level

1   Read every question carefully.

2   Answer all questions as fully as you can.

3   If you cannot do a question, go on to the next one. Try again later.

4   In question 3, answer **one** section only.

5   Write your answers in the answer book provided. Indicate clearly, in the left hand margin, the question and section of question being answered. Do not write in the right hand margin.

SCOTTISH
QUALIFICATIONS
AUTHORITY

SYLLABUS AREA 1—LIVING IN A DEMOCRACY

QUESTION 1

(a)

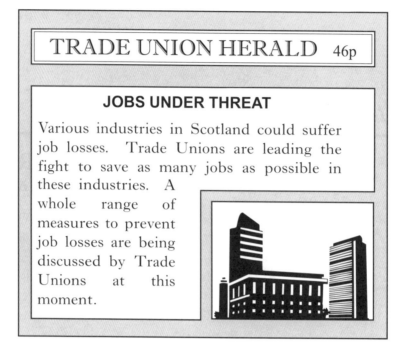

Describe, in detail, the **rights and responsibilities** of Trade Unions when trying to prevent job losses.

(Knowledge & Understanding, **6** marks)

QUESTION 1 (CONTINUED)

(b)   Study the information below, then answer the question which follows.

Workers' views of what Trade Unions should try to do (%)

Most common issues mentioned by workers	1989	1999
◆ Protect existing jobs	28	33
◆ Improve working conditions	21	21
◆ Improve pay	28	22
◆ Have more say over management long-term plans	6	7
◆ Reduce pay differences at workplace	6	4
◆ Have more say over how work is done day to day	3	2
◆ Women's issues	3	4
◆ Others	5	7

Women's issues, pay and working conditions are the issues of most concern to workers today just as they were ten years ago.

View of John Milligan

Using only the information above, explain why John Milligan could be accused of being **selective in his use of facts**.

(Enquiry Skills, **4** marks)

[Turn over

QUESTION 1 (CONTINUED)

(c)   Study Sources 1 and 2 below and opposite, then answer the question which follows.

Source 1
Breakdown of Seats in parts of Scotland
Members of the Scottish Parliament (MSPs)—breakdown by party in different parts of Scotland

Highlands and Islands

Party	C	R
Labour	1	3
SNP	2	2
Conservative	0	2
Liberal Democrat	5	0
Scottish Socialist	0	0
Green Party	0	0
Independent	0	0

Glasgow

Party	C	R
Labour	10	0
SNP	0	4
Conservative	0	1
Liberal Democrat	0	1
Scottish Socialist	0	1
Green Party	0	0
Independent	0	0

North East Scotland

Party	C	R
Labour	4	0
SNP	2	4
Conservative	0	3
Liberal Democrat	3	0
Scottish Socialist	0	0
Green Party	0	0
Independent	0	0

West of Scotland

Party	C	R
Labour	9	0
SNP	0	4
Conservative	0	2
Liberal Democrat	0	1
Scottish Socialist	0	0
Green Party	0	0
Independent	0	0

Mid Scotland and Fife

Party	C	R
Labour	6	0
SNP	2	3
Conservative	0	3
Liberal Democrat	1	1
Scottish Socialist	0	0
Green Party	0	0
Independent	0	0

Central Scotland

Party	C	R
Labour	9	0
SNP	0	5
Conservative	0	1
Liberal Democrat	0	1
Scottish Socialist	0	0
Green Party	0	0
Independent	1	0

South of Scotland

Party	C	R
Labour	6	0
SNP	1	3
Conservative	0	4
Liberal Democrat	2	0
Scottish Socialist	0	0
Green Party	0	0
Independent	0	0

Lothians

Party	C	R
Labour	8	0
SNP	0	3
Conservative	0	2
Liberal Democrat	1	1
Scottish Socialist	0	0
Green Party	0	1
Independent	0	0

C = Constituency   R = Regional List

QUESTION 1 (CONTINUED)

Source 2

Result of the 1999 Election to the Scottish Parliament				
Party	Percentage of votes cast for each party in constituencies	Number of constituency MSPs elected	Percentage of votes cast for each party in Regional List	Number of Regional List MSPs elected	Total number of MSPs
Labour	39%	53	33·8%	3	56
SNP	29%	7	27·5%	28	35
Liberal Democrat	14%	12	12·5%	5	17
Conservative	16%	0	15·4%	18	18
Green Party	0%	0	3·6%	1	1
Independent	1%	1	7·1%	0	1
Scottish Socialist	1%	0	0·1%	1	1
Totals		73		56	129

Using only the information in Sources 1 and 2 above and opposite, what **conclusions** can be reached about the **success of different political parties** at the election to the Scottish Parliament in 1999?

You must use information from both sources, and you must reach **at least three well-developed conclusions** in your answer.

(Enquiry Skills, **8** marks)

[Turn over

SYLLABUS AREA 2—CHANGING SOCIETY

QUESTION 2

(a)

> *Some families with young children have a better living standard than others.*

Explain, **in detail**, why *some families with young children have a better living standard than others.*

(Knowledge and Understanding, **6** marks)

(b)

> *Recent Government policies have helped many people move from benefits to work.*

Explain, **in detail**, the ways in which *recent Government policies have helped many people move from benefits to work.*

(Knowledge and Understanding, **4** marks)

(c)   Study Sources 1, 2 and 3 below and opposite, then answer the question which follows.

SOURCE 1

We agree with the Government and the trade unions that all workers in the UK are entitled to have a decent wage but the introduction of the Minimum Wage has created many problems for us. At a time when we are faced with severe competition due to the strength of the pound, we have been forced to put up wages and therefore our costs. This can only lead to job losses for some people.

As employers, we are interested in retaining good staff and even in traditionally low paid areas like check-out operators, many workers earn between £4 and £5 an hour. The UK does not need the introduction of a Minimum Wage as only 4.4% of part-time female workers earned less than £3.60 an hour in 1999. The Government should not interfere with the rights of employers to run their own businesses as they wish. After all, it is our businesses that create the wealth of this country. The natural forces of supply and demand will ensure that all share in its prosperity.

James Murray, Company Director

SOURCE 2

The introduction of the Minimum Wage in 1998 by the Labour Government has benefited many of our members. Before the Minimum Wage many workers were earning as little as £2.50 an hour and those with families were entitled to benefits paid by the Benefits Agency. In modern Britain, everyone is entitled to a decent wage but many still earn less than the amount agreed in Europe as the poverty line. Although some employers have cut jobs or working hours, employment actually grew in many low-paid industries. We urge the Government to continue to raise the Minimum Wage as current levels do not go far enough to meet the needs of low-paid workers and there are still too many employers who do not pay the agreed rates. People under 21 do not have enough protection with even lower rates or no minimum wage at all. It is important that the Government continues to play an important role in determining wages as employers are only interested in maximising their profits.

Eric Small, Shop Steward

QUESTION 2 (c) (CONTINUED)

SOURCE 3

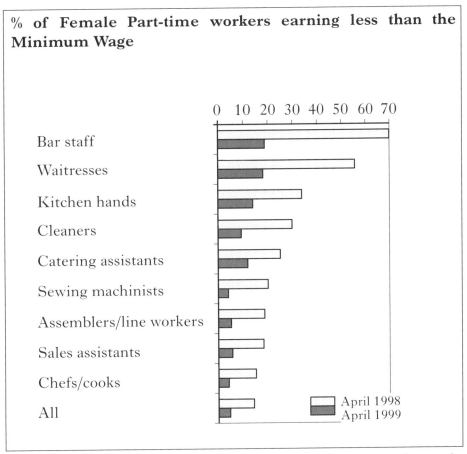

% of Female Part-time workers earning less than the Minimum Wage

Bar staff
Waitresses
Kitchen hands
Cleaners
Catering assistants
Sewing machinists
Assemblers/line workers
Sales assistants
Chefs/cooks
All

April 1998
April 1999

Source – *The Economist*

The introduction of the Minimum Wage has benefited all workers and employers in the UK.

Government Spokesperson

Using only Sources 1, 2 and 3 above and opposite, explain why the Government Spokesperson could be accused of being **selective in the use of facts**.

Your answer must be based entirely on Sources 1, 2 and 3.

(Enquiry Skills, **8** marks)

[Turn over

SYLLABUS AREA 3—IDEOLOGIES

QUESTION 3

Answer **ONE** Section only: Section (A)—The USA on pages *eight* and *nine*.

OR Section (B)—Russia on pages *ten* and *eleven*.

OR Section (C)—China on pages *twelve* and *thirteen*.

(A) **THE USA**

(a) | *American citizens can participate in elections.* |

Describe, **in detail**, two ways in which *American citizens can participate in elections*.

In your answer you must mention USA examples.

(Knowledge and Understanding, **4** marks)

(b) | In recent years *the living standards of many members of ethnic minority groups in the USA have improved*. |

Explain, **in detail**, why *the living standards of many members of ethnic minority groups in the USA have improved*.

In your answer you must mention USA examples.

(Knowledge and Understanding, **4** marks)

QUESTION 3(A) (CONTINUED)

You have been asked to carry out an investigation on the topic in the box below.

> **Equal opportunities for men and women in the USA.**

Now answer questions (c), (d), (e), (f) and (g).

(c) State a relevant **hypothesis** for your investigation.

(Enquiry Skills, **2** marks)

(d) Give **two aims or headings** to help you prove or disprove your hypothesis.

(Enquiry Skills, **2** marks)

(e) | You decide to use the internet to help with your investigation. |

Describe how you would find information using the **internet**.

(Enquiry Skills, **2** marks)

(f) Explain why using the **internet** would be a good method for this topic.

(Enquiry Skills, **2** marks)

(g) To help you carry out your investigation into "Equal Opportunities for Men and Women in the USA", your teacher gives you a **folder of newspaper cuttings** about the USA.

What problems might you have in using the information in the folder of newspaper cuttings about the USA?

(Enquiry Skills, **2** marks)

NOW GO TO QUESTION 4 ON PAGE FIFTEEN

QUESTION 3 (CONTINUED)

(B) **RUSSIA**

(a) | *Russian citizens can participate in elections.* |

Describe, **in detail**, two ways in which *Russian citizens can participate in elections*.

In your answer you must mention Russian examples.

(Knowledge and Understanding, **4** marks)

(b) | In recent years *the gap in living standards between rich and poor in Russia has widened.* |

Explain, **in detail**, why *the gap in living standards between rich and poor in Russia has widened*.

In your answer you must mention Russian examples.

(Knowledge and Understanding, **4** marks)

QUESTION 3(B) (CONTINUED)

You have been asked to carry out an investigation on the topic in the box below.

> **Equal opportunities for men and women in Russia.**

Now answer questions (c), (d), (e), (f) and (g).

(c)   State a relevant **hypothesis** for your investigation.

(Enquiry Skills, **2** marks)

(d)   Give **two aims or headings** to help you prove or disprove your hypothesis.

(Enquiry Skills, **2** marks)

(e) | You decide to use the internet to help with your investigation. |

Describe how you would find information using the **internet**.

(Enquiry Skills, **2** marks)

(f)   Explain why using the **internet** would be a good method for this topic.

(Enquiry Skills, **2** marks)

(g)   To help you carry out your investigation into "Equal Opportunities for Men and Women in Russia", your teacher gives you a **folder of newspaper cuttings** about Russia.

What problems might you have in using the information in the folder of newspaper cuttings about Russia?

(Enquiry Skill, **2** marks)

NOW GO TO QUESTION 4 ON PAGE FIFTEEN

QUESTION 3 (CONTINUED)

(C) **CHINA**

(a) | *Chinese citizens can participate in elections.* |

Describe, **in detail**, two ways in which *Chinese citizens can participate in elections.*

In your answer you must mention Chinese examples.

(Knowledge and Understanding, **4** marks)

(b) | In recent years *the gap in living standards between rich and poor in China has widened.* |

Explain, **in detail**, why *the gap in living standards between rich and poor in China has widened.*

In your answer you must mention Chinese examples.

(Knowledge and Understanding, **4** marks)

QUESTION 3(c) (CONTINUED)

You have been asked to carry out an investigation on the topic in the box below.

> **Equal opportunities for men and women in China.**

Now answer questions (c), (d), (e), (f) and (g).

(c)   State a relevant **hypothesis** for your investigation.

          (Enquiry Skills, **2** marks)

(d)   Give **two aims or headings** to help you prove or disprove your hypothesis.

          (Enquiry Skills, **2** marks)

(e)
> You decide to use the internet to help with your investigation.

Describe how you would find information using the **internet**.

          (Enquiry Skills, **2** marks)

(f)   Explain why using the **internet** would be a good method for this topic.

          (Enquiry Skills, **2** marks)

(g)   To help you carry out your investigation into "Equal Opportunities for Men and Women in China", your teacher gives you a **folder of newspaper cuttings** about China.

     What problems might you have in using the information in the folder of newspaper cuttings about China?

          (Enquiry Skills, **2** marks)

NOW GO TO QUESTION 4 ON PAGE FIFTEEN

[BLANK PAGE]

SYLLABUS AREA 4—INTERNATIONAL RELATIONS

QUESTION 4

(a)

| Debt crisis deepens | Cocoa prices collapse | Aid package announced |

European countries have power over some African countries. In what ways can European countries **benefit** from links with poorer countries in Africa?

In your answer you should refer to specific examples.

(Knowledge and Understanding, **8** marks)

[Turn over

QUESTION 4 (CONTINUED)

(b)   Study Sources 1, 2 and 3 below and opposite, then answer the question which follows.

SOURCE 1

SOUTH AFRICAN TIMES
Africa's Top English-Language Newspaper

FLOOD DISASTER
STRIKES MOZAMBIQUE

Tens of thousands of people are homeless after flooding hit the southern part of Mozambique. The Limpopo River burst its banks and flood water now covers hundreds of square kilometres of Mozambique's most fertile land. Many important road bridges have been swept away and some areas have been cut-off completely. Mozambique has appealed for aid to help rebuild the transport and communications system.

The most urgent problem is to rescue thousands of people who have become stranded on isolated areas of higher ground. Twelve rescue helicopters from South Africa and two from Zimbabwe were able to reach the scene and saved hundreds of people from the water itself, from the tops of trees and from the roofs of buildings. A Mozambique government minister made a plea for more help from the outside world. "Thousands of people have been drowned, but many more will die unless they are rescued quickly and moved to higher ground. The forecast is for more rain over the next week, and people who think they are safe could still be in real danger."

One survivor, plucked from the dirty waters of the swollen Limpopo River said "I owe my life to the bravery and skill of the helicopter pilot and winchman."

SOURCE 2

Mozambique

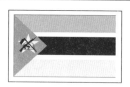

Population: 17·8 million
Capital City: Maputo
GNP per head: $80
Economic Growth Rate
(1999): 7% (fastest in
Africa)

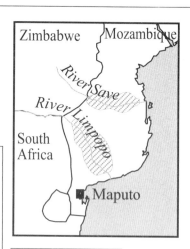

Zimbabwe   Mozambique

River Save

River Limpopo

South
Africa

Maputo

▨ Flooded Land

The World Food Programme had about 8000 tonnes of food stockpiled in Mozambique, but had problems distributing it. Roads and railways were wrecked by the floods, making it difficult to transport food to remote areas. Within days of the disaster there were 60 helicopters operating in Mozambique, but the International Red Cross said there still were not enough to do the job.

Flooding along the Limpopo and Save Rivers was amongst the worst ever seen in Africa. More than two weeks of storms followed by the arrival of Cyclone Eline left a trail of damage across Southern Africa.

Mozambique's main army base is in Maputo, the capital city. The army has a small number of small assault helicopters. There are no large personnel carrying helicopters.

QUESTION 4 (CONTINUED)

SOURCE 3

Disaster in Africa

No-one could have known how bad the floods would become. The extraordinary pictures of people being plucked from trees sparked enormous interest and public support – the British public gave over 13 million pounds in the week following the disaster.

Some of the planes flying over Mozambique could not land where the help was most needed.

"Why are troops not mending the roads?" asked The Guardian newspaper. The main road from Maputo to the north was impassable in at least five places, yet was vital for the distribution of food, medicines and other supplies.

Mozambique needs emergency help. With transport links broken, something has to be done quickly to get supplies to remote parts of the country. People will die unless food, water and medicines are moved quickly.

Immediate needs:

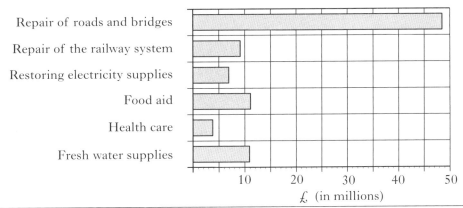

Adapted from the Oxfam and the Agencia Informacao Mozambique Websites

The UK is considering how to help with the crisis in Mozambique. The government intends to spend £15 million on aid. They are considering **two options**.

Option 1 – UK sends helicopters and pilots to Mozambique. It will take 7 days until they get there. Capabilities – search and rescue, transporting people, food and materials.	**Option 2** – UK sends team of engineers to Mozambique. It will take 2 weeks until they get there. Capabilities – bridge and road building, erecting temporary buildings, re-connecting electricity and water supplies.

Using only information from Sources 1, 2 and 3 on pages *sixteen* and *seventeen*, **explain which option you would recommend for the British government**.

Give detailed reasons to support your recommendation.

(Enquiry Skills, **8** marks)

(c)   Give **one reason** to explain why you have rejected the other option.

(Enquiry Skills, **2** marks)

[END OF QUESTION PAPER]

[BLANK PAGE]

C

2640/403

NATIONAL
QUALIFICATIONS
2002

THURSDAY, 30 MAY
1.00 PM – 3.00 PM

MODERN STUDIES
STANDARD GRADE
Credit Level

1   Read every question carefully.

2   Answer all questions as fully as you can.

3   If you cannot do a question, go on to the next one. Try again later.

4   In question 3, answer **one** section only.

5   Write your answers in the answer book provided. Indicate clearly, in the left hand margin, the question and section of question being answered. Do not write in the right hand margin.

SCOTTISH
QUALIFICATIONS
AUTHORITY

[BLANK PAGE]

SYLLABUS AREA 1—LIVING IN A DEMOCRACY

QUESTION 1

(a) | *"MSPs **represent** their constituents in the Scottish Parliament."*

Describe, **in detail**, the ways in which *MSPs **represent** their constituents in the Scottish Parliament.*

(Knowledge & Understanding, **6** marks)

[Turn over

QUESTION 1 (CONTINUED)

(*b*)   Study the information about Marchglen on *page five* opposite. Also study the information in Sources 1 and 2 below. Sources 1 and 2 contain information about the two people on the short-list to become Labour candidate for Marchglen.

Answer the question on *page five*.

SOURCE 1

Profile of Jean Alder

Jean previously worked as election agent for an unsuccessful Labour candidate. She is 55 years of age and has been a Labour Party member for 25 years.

Jean was born in London and lived there until she moved to Marchglen four years ago. Jean spent 20 years working for a major Trade Union. She earned a reputation as a tough negotiator and has experience of dealing with factory closures.

Jean's main interests apart from politics include history and gardening. She enjoys travelling and has visited Japan several times. She is married and has two grown-up children.

Extract from a campaign speech:

"I would like to see better public transport. More government money should be spent on re-training people who have lost their jobs. New skills are the key to better wage levels and living standards. We should not give help to foreign companies unless they guarantee to stay in Scotland for at least ten years—many leave when economic conditions change."

SOURCE 2

Profile of Jennifer Wood

Jennifer was born and brought up in Marchglen. Now 38 years of age, she became involved in politics 8 years ago. She has been a Local Councillor on Marchglen Council for the last four years. Two years ago she visited America and helped to attract an American computer assembly company to Marchglen, creating 400 jobs.

At the last General Election Jennifer was the election agent for a successful Labour candidate in the neighbouring constituency of Sandyknowe. Jennifer is very interested in environmental issues. She has also taken part in anti fox-hunting demonstrations.

Jennifer works as a vet but would give up her job to go into politics full-time if she became MP. She spent six years working abroad and is fluent in three foreign languages, including Japanese.

Extract from a campaign speech:

"I would like to see more encouragement for small businesses—they are the key to providing jobs in the future. We must also clean up our local environment by cutting pollution—electricity should be provided from wind-power generators. I also think that all people deserve a decent wage—too many people in Marchglen are paid low wages. I would campaign to raise the National Minimum Wage to £5 per hour."

QUESTION 1 (*b*) (CONTINUED)

Information about Marchglen constituency

- Marchglen is a constituency in Central Scotland. It is an area where traditional industries such as coal mining have closed down putting 2000 people out of work. Some new industries, including a call centre and a computer assembly plant, have been established. 80,000 people live in the constituency.

- Unemployment remains a major problem—the level is twice the average for Scotland. Wage levels in some of the new industries in Marchglen are below the national average.

- The biggest "traditional" employer is a large textile factory—but the American company which owns it has threatened to close it within the next two years. 1500 jobs could be lost.

- Environmental issues are important due to concerns about pollution from a chemical waste disposal plant in Marchglen. Local people have campaigned to have the railway to Marchglen re-opened. It was closed in the 1960s.

- At the last General Election the seat was won by Labour. However, they lost the seat to the SNP at a by-election two years ago. The SNP had a small majority of 306 at the by-election compared to a Labour majority of 5497 at the last General Election.

- The Scottish Executive and the local council have set up "Project Marchglen" to try and attract more foreign businesses to the area. A large Japanese company is considering opening a mobile phone factory in the constituency.

(*b*) (i) Using only the information about Marchglen and Sources 1 and 2 above and opposite, explain which person would be the most suitable to be selected by the Labour Party as their candidate for this constituency at the next General Election.

Give **detailed** reasons to explain your choice.

In your answer you must relate information about the candidates to the information about the constituency.

(Enquiry Skills, **6** marks)

(ii) **Explain** why you rejected the other candidate.

(Enquiry Skills, **2** marks)

[Turn over

QUESTION 1 (CONTINUED)

(c)   Study Sources 1 and 2 below, then answer the question which follows.

SOURCE 1

Scottish Parliament (2001)—MSPs by Party and Gender			
Party	Members of the Scottish Parliament (MSPs)		
	Male	Female	Total
Labour	28	28	56
SNP	20	15	35
Conservative	15	3	18
Liberal Democrat	15	2	17
Scottish Socialist	1	0	1
Green Party	1	0	1
Independent	1	0	1
Total	**81**	**48**	**129**

SOURCE 2

UK Parliament (after 2001 General Election)—Scottish MPs by Party and Gender			
Party	Members of Parliament (MPs)		
	Male	Female	Total
Labour	45	11	56
Conservative	1	0	1
Liberal Democrat	10	0	10
SNP	4	1	5
Total	**60**	**12**	**72**

> "Women are well represented amongst Scotland's MPs and MSPs. This is true for all parties."

View of Jane Smith

Using Sources 1 and 2 above, explain why Jane Smith could be accused of being **selective in her use of facts**.

Use only information from Sources 1 and 2 in your answer.

(Enquiry Skills, **4** marks)

SYLLABUS AREA 2—CHANGING SOCIETY

QUESTION 2

(a) | Some elderly people have greater health **needs** than other elderly people.

Explain, **in detail**, why *some elderly people have greater health* **needs** *than other elderly people.*

(Knowledge and Understanding, **6** marks)

(b) | Some people believe that the government should increase the level of the old age pension.

Explain, **in detail**, why *some people believe that the government should increase the level of the old age pension.*

(Knowledge and Understanding, **4** marks)

[Turn over

QUESTION 2 (CONTINUED)

(c)   Study Sources 1and 2 below and opposite, then answer the question which follows.

SOURCE 1

Statistical Information—Accommodation for Elderly People in Scotland (1990 – 1999)			
	1990	**1995**	**1999**
Special Needs Housing (Number of dwellings)			
Very Sheltered Housing	n/a	671	1,620
Sheltered Housing	26,737	33,687	36,708
Adapted Housing	10,456	19,013	20,216
(Total)	(37,193)	(53,371)	(58,544)
Residential Care Homes (Number of places)			
Local Authority	8,807	7,584	6,059
Private	3,195	3,934	4,477
Voluntary	4,335	3,807	3,684
(Total)	(16,337)	(15,325)	(14,220)
Private Nursing Homes (Number of places)	12,866	15,986	20,188
NHS Hospital Beds in Scotland			
Geriatric Long-stay (Residential)	9,277	7,729	4,924
Geriatric Short-stay (Assessment)	2,521	3,245	3,634
(Total)	(11,798)	(10,974)	(8,558)

Source – *Scottish Community Care Statistics, 1999*

QUESTION 2 (c) (CONTINUED)

SOURCE 2

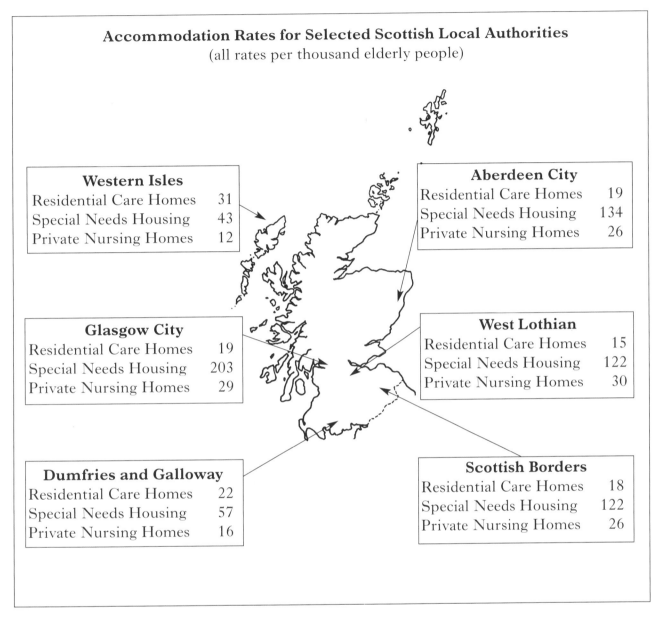

Accommodation Rates for Selected Scottish Local Authorities
(all rates per thousand elderly people)

Western Isles
Residential Care Homes	31
Special Needs Housing	43
Private Nursing Homes	12

Aberdeen City
Residential Care Homes	19
Special Needs Housing	134
Private Nursing Homes	26

Glasgow City
Residential Care Homes	19
Special Needs Housing	203
Private Nursing Homes	29

West Lothian
Residential Care Homes	15
Special Needs Housing	122
Private Nursing Homes	30

Dumfries and Galloway
Residential Care Homes	22
Special Needs Housing	57
Private Nursing Homes	16

Scottish Borders
Residential Care Homes	18
Special Needs Housing	122
Private Nursing Homes	26

Using only the information in Sources 1 and 2 above and opposite, what **conclusions** can be reached about **accommodation for elderly people** in Scotland?

You must use information from **all** the sources.

You should reach conclusions about the following.

- Accommodation rates in different parts of Scotland

- Ways in which accommodation for elderly people has changed since 1990

- Number **and** use of NHS hospital beds

- Relationship between NHS hospital beds and other types of accommodation

(Enquiry Skills, **8** marks)

[Turn over

SYLLABUS AREA 3—IDEOLOGIES

QUESTION 3

Answer **ONE** Section only: Section (A)—The USA on pages *ten* and *eleven*.

                                   OR Section (B)—Russia on pages *twelve* and *thirteen*.

                                   OR Section (C)—China on pages *fourteen* and *fifteen*.

(A) **THE USA**

(a) | *The American people have* **political rights and responsibilities.** |
        |---|

Describe, **in detail**, the **political rights** of *American people* **and** the **responsibilities** that go with them.

In your answer you **must** refer to American examples.

                                       (Knowledge and Understanding, **8** marks)

QUESTION 3(A) (CONTINUED)

You have been asked to carry out an investigation on the topic below.

Equality in the USA

Now answer questions (*b*), (*c*), (*d*), (*e*) and (*f*).

(*b*)   State a relevant **hypothesis** for your investigation.

(Enquiry Skills, **2** marks)

(*c*)   Give **two aims or headings** to help you prove or disprove your hypothesis.

(Enquiry Skills, **2** marks)

You decide to use a variety of sources to help with your investigation into this topic.

(*d*)   Describe how you would find relevant **web sites** to help with your investigation.

(Enquiry Skills, **2** marks)

(*e*)   Explain why using **e-mail** would be a good method of enquiry for this topic.

(Enquiry Skills, **2** marks)

(*f*)   To help you carry out your investigation, your teacher gives you a **collection of Encyclopedias on 4 CD-ROMs**.

What **problems** might you have in using the information in the **collection of Encyclopedias on 4 CD-ROMs**?

(Enquiry Skills, **2** marks)

NOW GO TO QUESTION 4 ON PAGE SEVENTEEN

QUESTION 3 (CONTINUED)

(B) **RUSSIA**

(a)

> *Since the break-up of the Soviet Union, Russians have enjoyed more **political rights and responsibilities**.*

Describe, **in detail**, the ***political rights and responsibilities*** now *enjoyed* by *Russians*.

In your answer you **must** refer to Russian examples.

(Knowledge and Understanding, **8** marks)

QUESTION 3(B) (CONTINUED)

You have been asked to carry out an investigation on the topic below.

Equality in Russia

Now answer questions (*b*), (*c*), (*d*), (*e*) and (*f*).

(*b*)   State a relevant **hypothesis** for your investigation.

(Enquiry Skills, **2** marks)

(*c*)   Give **two aims or headings** to help you prove or disprove your hypothesis.

(Enquiry Skills, **2** marks)

You decide to use a variety of sources to help with your investigation into this topic.

(*d*)   Describe how you would find relevant **web sites** to help with your investigation.

(Enquiry Skills, **2** marks)

(*e*)   Explain why using **e-mail** would be a good method of enquiry for this topic.

(Enquiry Skills, **2** marks)

(*f*)   To help you carry out your investigation, your teacher gives you a **collection of Encyclopedias on 4 CD-ROMs**.

What **problems** might you have in using the information in the **collection of Encyclopedias on 4 CD-ROMs**?

(Enquiry Skill, **2** marks)

NOW GO TO QUESTION 4 ON PAGE SEVENTEEN

QUESTION 3 (CONTINUED)

(C) **CHINA**

(a)

> *Many Chinese people want more **political rights**.*

Describe, **in detail**, the arguments used by *Chinese people* who *want more **political rights***.

In your answer you **must** refer to Chinese examples.

(Knowledge and Understanding, **8** marks)

QUESTION 3 (c) (CONTINUED)

 You have been asked to carry out an investigation on the topic below.

> **Equality in China**

Now answer questions (b), (c), (d), (e) and (f).

(b)   State a relevant **hypothesis** for your investigation.

(Enquiry Skills, **2** marks)

(c)   Give **two aims or headings** to help you prove or disprove your hypothesis.

(Enquiry Skills, **2** marks)

You decide to use a variety of sources to help with your investigation into this topic.

(d)   Describe how you would find relevant **web sites** to help with your investigation.

(Enquiry Skills, **2** marks)

(e)   Explain why using **e-mail** would be a good method of enquiry for this topic.

(Enquiry Skills, **2** marks)

(f)   To help you carry out your investigation, your teacher gives you a **collection of Encyclopedias on 4 CD-ROMs**.

What **problems** might you have in using the information in the **collection of Encyclopedias on 4 CD-ROMs**?

(Enquiry Skills, **2** marks)

NOW GO TO QUESTION 4 ON PAGE SEVENTEEN

[BLANK PAGE]

SYLLABUS AREA 4—INTERNATIONAL RELATIONS

QUESTION 4

(a)

> The United Nations has used its **power** to intervene in recent conflicts in Europe.

Choose **one** recent conflict in Europe that you have studied.

Describe, **in detail**, the role of the *United Nations* during the conflict you have chosen.

(Knowledge and Understanding, **4** marks)

(b)

> Some countries in Eastern Europe feel that their **needs** would be met through joining NATO.

Explain, **in detail**, why *some countries in Eastern Europe feel that their* **needs** *would be met through joining NATO.*

(Knowledge and Understanding, **4** marks)

[Turn over

QUESTION 4 (CONTINUED)

(c)   Study Sources 1, 2, 3 and 4 below and opposite, then answer the question which follows.

SOURCE 1

Britain must join the Euro

Why are the British people so hesitant and negative about the Single European Currency (Euro)? Is it because they are too narrow-minded? Do they have a fear of things foreign? Do they just love the pound? Whatever it is, it isn't based on real facts. The media refuses to highlight all the positives that will come from joining. It will protect jobs and keep prices steady throughout the EU. There is no reason to believe that the British people will lose their national identity—the UK will remain an independent country in Europe.

Sometimes British people find it hard to get excited about Europe. The fact is that Britain needs Europe and our partners in the European Union. More than 70% of UK exports go to European Union countries. This is what British prosperity has been built upon. Surely we want this to continue? The only way for this to happen is to join the Single European Currency and enjoy the benefits which it will bring.

Statement by Pro European Businessman

SOURCE 2

Eurobarometer Opinion Poll

Please state whether you Agree or Disagree with the following statement:

There has to be one single currency, the Euro, replacing the National Currencies of the member states of the European Union.

	Agree 1999	Agree 2000	Disagree 1999	Disagree 2000	Don't know 1999	Don't know 2000
*Germany	55	50	36	39	9	10
*Spain	72	75	18	18	10	7
*France	64	67	32	29	4	4
*Ireland	78	63	13	22	9	15
*Finland	47	49	49	48	4	3
UK	25	22	59	61	16	17

*Members of the Single European Currency, 2001.

SOURCE 3

What Europeans think joining the Euro will mean for them (%)	Yes	No	Don't know
• Create more jobs	42	36	22
• Cause countries to lose too much of their national identity	25	49	26
• Make it easier for people to travel	52	32	16
• Reduce differences between the rich and not quite so rich countries of the EU	22	53	25
• Increase crime levels due to increase in fake notes and coins	61	24	15
• Lead to rising bank charges	76	18	6

QUESTION 4 (c) (CONTINUED)

SOURCE 4

We love the pound

The British economy is booming. Unemployment is at a record low and Britain is the envy of the rest of Europe. Why would we want to throw this away by joining the Euro? The pound is stable and inflation is low. Figures show that the value of the Euro has gone down. This worries me. It would cost billions of pounds for all British businesses to change their systems to the Euro and only a small proportion would benefit from the reduced costs of trade with Europe. Why would we want to give it up? The EU has already taken away many of the powers that we had. Do we really want Brussels to set our Interest and Tax Rates? If we join the Euro, then we will have taken a massive step down the road to giving up our national identity. This is unthinkable for the British people.

(View of Businessman opposed to EURO membership.)

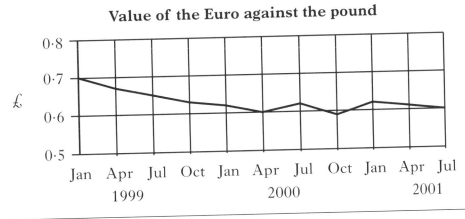

The United Kingdom should join the Single European Currency (Euro).

Using only the information from Sources 1, 2, 3 and 4 above and opposite, give arguments **for** and **against** the proposal that *the United Kingdom should join the Single European Currency (Euro).*

You should only use information from the Sources in your answer.

(Enquiry Skills, **8** marks)

(d)   Overall, do you support the proposal? **Explain** why you have reached this decision.

(Enquiry Skills, **2** marks)

[END OF QUESTION PAPER]

[BLANK PAGE]

[BLANK PAGE]

Leckie & Leckie has made every effort to trace all copyright holders. If any have been inadvertently overlooked, Leckie & Leckie will be pleased to make the necessary arrangements. Leckie & Leckie would like to thank the following for their permission to reproduce their material:

Pulse Publications for an extract from *The USA* by Clarke and Morrison (p 9);
The Independent for the extract *The results of the 1997 General Election in Scotland* (p 16);
The extract *Party support by housing and trade union membership* © (Copyright) Times Newspapers Limited, 1997 (p 75);
The extract *Has Peace Come to Chechnya?* Source: *The Economist* © The Economist Newspaper Limited, London 1996 (p 81);
Blackwell Publishers for the extract *Living Conditions in Russia Today* (p 96).

The following companies/individuals have very generously given permission to reproduce their copyright material free of charge:

An extract © 1996 Time Inc. Reprinted by permission (p 8);
One Parent Families Scotland for two extracts (p 18);
Vocational Technologies Ltd, 3rd Floor, 1 Pickford Street, Aldershot, GU11 1TY, (www.europeintheround.com) for an extract (p 26);
The extract *Immigration – an issue in the 1996 presidential election campaign* © 1996 Time Inc. Reprinted by permission (p 78);
Causeway Press Limited for an extract from *British Politics* by David Roberts (p 90);
The International Monetary Fund for an extract from their website (p 94);
The extract *Answers to Opinion Poll of US Citizens* © 1996 Time Inc. Reprinted by permission (p 95);
Asian Demographics Ltd for an extract (p 98);
The New Internationalist (www.newint.org) for the extract *Statistics on different regions in China* (p 100);
Age Concern England for an extract (p 108);
The Mozambique News Agency and Oxfam GB (www.oxfam.org.uk) for an extract from the Oxfam website (p 141);
Her Majesty's Stationery Office for an extract from *Scottish Community Care Statistics* (p 150).

Pocket answer section for
SQA Modern Studies Standard Grade
General and Credit Levels 1998 to 2002

Published by Leckie & Leckie Ltd, 8 Whitehill Terrace, St Andrews, Scotland, KY16 8RN
tel: 01334 475656, fax: 01334 477392, hq@leckieandleckie.co.uk, www.leckieandleckie.co.uk

Modern Studies
General Level
1998

1. (a) The skill being assessed is the ability of candidates to detect exaggeration and provide valid explanations.

    "Good points" include:

    • Membership has not remained constant. It has fallen in all 3 Trade Unions

    • Strikes have not continued to rise. There have been ups and downs with the latest year showing a reduction

   (b) The concept being assessed is **Participation**. Candidates are required to provide detailed explanations.

    "Good points" include:

    • Become a Shop Steward

    • Go along to Union meetings

    • Vote at elections for Trade Union posts, eg General Secretary

   (c) The skill being assessed is the ability of candidates to make comparisons between sources and draw **conclusions**.

    "Good points" include:

    • Strike action is the only way of finally resolving a dispute according to source 1, whereas source 2 believes that negotiation is the way forward as both sides suffer during strike

    • One feeling is that employers cannot be trusted whereas others accept shared interests between employers and workers

    • Source 1—believes employers increase profits at the workers expense whereas source 2 believes in productivity deals leading to better pay and conditions

   (d) The concept is **Representation**. Candidates should explain how factors interact.

    "Good points" include:

    • Raising matters in debates

    • Contacting officials

    • Contacts with other councillors eg committee chairs

    • Committee work

    • Leading demonstrations/campaigns

    • Discussions with local business interests

2. (a) The skill being assessed is the ability of candidates to support or oppose a given point of view.

    Evidence to support the view:

    "Good points" include:

    Andrew Hunt and Sons to make 150 of their workforce redundant due to the introduction of new technology

    Evidence to oppose the view:

    "Good points" include:

    Bytecorp's development will bring 500 new jobs to Scotland

   (b) The concept being assessed is **Need**. Candidates are required to explain how various factors interact.

    "Good points" include:

    • Current schemes aimed specifically at young people—Skillseekers etc

    • Labour's "New Deal" policies

    • Jobcentres and other measures not aimed specifically at young people are also acceptable, as they may help young people to find employment

    • Government policies to attract foreign investment to Scotland to create new jobs

    • any other valid point

    accept careers service

   (c) The skill being assessed is the ability of candidates to detect **exaggeration** and provide valid explanations.

    "Good points" include:

    • Child Benefit is paid to all families with children under 16, but Janet Adam wrongly states that benefits only go to the poorest families

    • A total of 6.9 million families benefit from Government help. Janet Adam states that "few families with children get any help from the Government"

   (d) The concept being assessed is **Equality**. Candidates are required to explain how various factors interact.

    "Good points" include:

    • Family commitments may mean that they have to take part-time work

    • Family commitments may mean that they are confined to working close to home

    • Lack of child-care facilities (creches, childminders) may restrict their access to employment

    • Some single parents may face discrimination from prospective employers

    • any other valid point

Modern Studies
General Level
1998 (cont.)

A—THE USA

3. (a) The concept being assessed is **Participation**. Candidates are required to provide detailed explanations.

"Good points" include:

- Freedom to organise and set up political movements in opposition to the government

- Threat to withdraw vote from governing party

- Ability to use free press and television to mobilise opposition to government

- Variety of political movements to join

- Right to stand for election in opposition to government

- Opportunity to vote for a choice of political parties

- Regular democratic elections at federal and local levels at which opposition may be expressed

- Right to lobby and campaign against government

- Right to free speech, freedom of assembly, right to use peaceful methods of protest

(b) The skill being assessed is the ability of candidates to detect **exaggeration** and provide valid esplanations.

"Good points" include:

- most people will not be pleased since Clinton only received 49% of the vote, this is less than half of those who voted

- most people will not be pleased since more people voted for candidates other than the winner, ie 51% combined vote for Dole and Perot as against only 49% for Clinton

- most whites will not be pleased since 46% voted for Dole, more than the 43% who voted for Clinton

- most men will not be pleased since as many voted for Dole as for Clinton at 44% each, less than half voted for Clinton

(c) The concept being assessed is **Rights and Responsibilities**. Candidates are required to explain how various factors interact.

"Good points" include:

- Right to Vote—voters have responsibility to register to vote, to consider the arguments of the various candidates, use right by casting vote in elections

- Right to own guns—gun owners have responsibility to keep gun secure, not to leave loaded, not to use in connection with illegal purposes, not to allow to fall into criminal hands

A 3. (a) continued

- Right to own property—property owners have responsibility to employ others on fair terms not to break employment laws, not to exploit customers/clients

- Right to a fair trial—those on trial have responsibility to tell the truth, not to interfere in the legal process eg intimidating witnesses, destroying evidence

(d) The skill being assessed is the ability of candidates to **support a given point of view**.

"Good points" include:

- while whites are more likely to be arrested for burglary than blacks, blacks are more likely to be arrested for both robbery and murder than whites, 61% of arrests for robbery are blacks as against only 38% for whites and 55% of arrests for murder are of blacks as against only 43% for whites

- although blacks only make up 12% of the population of the USA, their arrest rate for all three crimes is disproportionately high viz 29% of arrests for burglary, 61% of arrests for robbery and 55% of arrests for murder

B—RUSSIA

3. (a) The concept being assessed is **Participation**. Candidates are required to provide detailed explanations.

"Good points" include:

- People can now demonstrate against government policy

- People can now use the media

- People can campaign for alternative parties

- People can join pressure groups etc

(b) The skill being assessed is the ability of candidates to detect **exaggeration** and provide valid explanations.

"Good points" include:

- Yeltsin only got 35% of the vote in the first ballot. A second ballot was needed

- Opinion polls showed that Yeltsin was trusted by only 27% of the population

(c) The concept being assessed is **Rights and Responsibilities**. Candidates are required to explain how various factors interact.

"Good points" include:

- People are now allowed to set up their own businesses

- People can earn higher wages and bonuses

- Farmers can sell in private markets

Relate the above to improvements in living standards, eg better housing, more choice of foreign goods in the shops etc.

B 3. (*d*) The skill being assessed is the ability of the candidate to support a given point of view.

Award up to **two** marks for each reason, depending on the quality of argument and evidence used.

"Good points" include:

- Crime has increased by nine times since 1985; violent crime up; police ineffective
- Reported crime by children has increased from 112,000 in 1991 to 140,000 in 1996

C—CHINA

3. (*a*) The concept being assessed is **Participation**. Candidates are required to provide detailed explanations.

"Good points" include:

- the Communist Party does not allow political protests and demonstrations
- the Chinese government is willing to use the army against any protests or demonstrations against government policy
- the Communist Party does not allow other opposition groups so a different view cannot be given of government policy
- dissidents are treated very harshly by the Chinese government eg beatings, torture, house arrest, arbitrary imprisonment etc
- the mass media is tightly controlled by the Chinese government and so cannot protest about government policy
- the "big four rights" [to speak out freely, to air views freely, to hold debates, to write big character posters] were removed from the constitution in 1980 making it more difficult for people to protest against the government

(*b*) The skill being assessed is the ability of candidates to detect **exaggeration** provide valid explanations.

"Good points" include:

Source 1

- the 1987 law allowing villages to have their own elections
- by 1997 95% of villages has held their own elections

Source 2

- China has a higher % of women in Parliament than the UK or USA

The candidate may also mention that Han Suyun says there is no democracy in China, and women are poorly represented in Parliament in China.

(*c*) The concept being assessed is **Rights and Responsibilities**. Candidates are required to explain how various factors interact.

"Good points" include:

- right to own farm land, the growth of the Responsibility System in farming means peasants can choose what and how much they produce
- right to sell extra produced in private markets means peasants can choose what to sell and at what price to sell them
- right to build a privately owned house on farm land
- right to set up "sideline" business and keep any profits
- right of some workers to move from rural areas to urban areas for better paid work
- right of workers to work extra hours or not
- right of firms to choose what goods to produce and at what price to sell them; etc and so improve their living standards

(*d*) The skill being assessed is the ability of the candidate to express support for a given point of view.

"Good points" include:

- in some areas baby girls are drowned or abandoned
- baby girls will often be left outside an orphanage
- child deaths are lower for girls than boys in India or Pakistan

4. (*a*) The skill being assessed is the ability to make comparisons within a source and draw conclusions.

"Good points" include:

For Guinea

- infant deaths are higher than those in Malawi
- life expectancy is lower than in Malawi

For Malawi

- the birth rate is higher than that in Guinea
- average annual income is lower than in Guinea.

(*b*) The concept being assessed is **Power**. Candidates are required to provide detailed explanations.

"Good points" include:

- the country receiving the aid may have to spend it on the European country's equipment
- the country receiving the aid may feel obligated to give the European country political, military, strategic or economic support
- the country receiving the aid may have to sell its cash crop at a price fixed by the European country
- the conditions of the aid may secure jobs in the donor country, etc.

Modern Studies
General Level
1998 (cont.)

4. (c)   The skill being assessed is the ability of candidates to support a given point of view.

"Good points" include:

- farming land has been taken and there may be food shortages in the future
- 1000 families have been displaced
- 500 construction jobs only last for three years
- the 100 permanent jobs only go to locals who can speak English

(d)   The concept being assessed is **Need**. Candidates are required to provide detailed explanations.

Credit highly candidates who display specific knowledge of programmes/agencies in particular parts of Africa.

"Good points" include:

UNICEF

food in emergencies
health and hygiene training for mothers
breastfeeding programmes
aid to refugees/orphans

WHO

immunisation programmes
medical and nursing training
provision of clinics and medicines
medical research

FAO

provision of tools, machinery for farmers
provision of drought, pest/disease resistant seeds
training in appropriate farming methods
research into better food production
improved food storage irrigation

UNESCO

literacy campaigns
provision of educational materials eg books, translation
aims of universal schooling especially for girls
teacher training
provision of education relevant to local African conditions

Modern Studies
General Level
1999

1. (a)   The concept being assessed is **Representation**. Candidates are required to provide detailed explanations.

"Good points" include:

- Listening to constituents problems/points of view during the MPs surgery
- Writing letters on behalf of constituents
- Conveying constituents views to the floor of the House of Commons
- Speaking in debates
- Bringing on-stream a Private Members Bill

(b)   The skill being assessed is the ability of candidates to support a given point of view.

"Good points" include:

- If they changed then they would be guaranteed seats in any parliament as the number of seats depends on the percentage of the vote gained, eg 18% of the popular vote would guarantee them 18% of the seats in a Scottish Parliament
- Parties such as the Liberal Democrats would not get so many seats under the new system. 13% of the vote got them 10 seats in Scotland which is out of proportion to their popularity in the country overall
- It would also ensure that no one party could get a majority of seats without getting a majority of the votes cast. This happened in 1997 with the Labour party

(c)   The skill being assessed is the ability of candidates to make comparisons within a source and draw conclusions.

"Good points" include:

- The number of women elected to parliament has doubled to 120 in 1997
- By far the biggest increase is in the Labour party
- The number of women standing as candidates has fallen substantially from a high of 568, to 372 in 1997
- Over 10 year period women candidates have increased

(d)   The skill being assessed is the ability of candidates to detect exaggeration and provide valid explanations.

"Good points" include:

- This is exaggerated in that, in the Welsh referendum, the Yes/No split was extremely close
- In Scotland, turnout was over 60% which is more than half the electorate

2. (*a*) The concept being assessed is **Equality**. Candidates are required to provide detailed explanations.

"Good points" include:

- Means-tested benefits targeted at the less well-off families
- Specific payments for Lone-Parent Families
- Extra payments for families caring for disabled people
- Some better-off families receive no benefit payments

Credit reference to any other valid points

(*b*) The skill being assessed is the ability of candidates to detect exaggeration and provide valid explanations.

"Good points" include:

From Source 1:

Since the CSA was set up more than 15,000 single parent families have been taken off benefit

From Source 2:

The average weekly maintenance payment has increased from £26.81 to £43.46 since the CSA was set up

(*c*) The concept being assessed is **Need**. Candidates are required to provide detailed explanations.

"Good points" include:

- Correlation between old age and incidence of specific acute conditions
- Correlation between old age and various chronic conditions
- Elderly people may be unable to look after themselves when they are ill
- Elderly people may have no family/relatives to look after them when they are ill

Credit any other valid points

(*d*) The skill being assessed is the ability of candidates to make comparisons within a source and draw conclusions.

"Good points" include:

For Site A

- Next to Post Office for collecting pensions
- Next to Health Centre—elderly people make more use of health services than other groups
- Near Church—important to many elderly people

Against Site A

- Close to Youth Club—potential noise and nuisance
- Close to Fire Station—potential disturbance
- No pedestrian access to Post Office

2. (*d*) **continued**

For Site B

- Next to Bowling Green—popular pursuit of elderly people
- Pedestrian Crossing link to small local shops—popular with older people. Also near shopping centre
- Close to Community Centre—possible venue for events for elderly people

Against Site B

- Next to High School—likelihood of noise and disturbance
- Drug rehab centre—may worry old people
- Near football ground—traffic, noise

Credit any other valid points

A—THE USA

3. (*a*) The concept being assessed is **Participation**. Candidates are required to provide detailed explanations.

"Good points" include:

- All American citizens have the opportunity to vote for the President in a nationwide election to the post of head of the Federal level of government every 4 years
- Americans in each state have the opportunity to vote for 2 Senators who will represent their interests in the Senate/Congress every 6 years
- Americans in each district have the opportunity to vote for a Member of the House of Representatives who will represent their interests in House of Representatives/Congress every 2 years
- Americans in each state have the opportunity to vote for a Govenor who will be the head of government at state level—usually every 4 years
- At the city/local level, Americans have the right to vote for a range of representatives including mayors, city councillors and a range of other local officials

Accept other examples of participation in the electoral process eg campaigns

(*b*) The concept being assessed is **Ideology**. Candidates are required to explain how various factors interact.

"Good points" include:

- American constitution guarantees the rights to freedom of speech and freedom of the press. These rights are incompatible with government control of the media
- In a democratic society such as USA it is important that government is accountable to the public and that the public have the information to make informed judgements through an independent press

Modern Studies
General Level
1999 (cont.)

A 3. (b) continued

- America is a capitalist society with private ownership of business, including media, private owners of newspapers and electronic media would not be happy with government control/censorship
- American media has had many examples of exposing government wrongdoing from Watergate through to Clinton "scandals"
- There is a vast number of different media, print and electronic, it would be practically very difficult for the government to control so many different media outlets

(c) (i) Candidates are required to state **one** aim/heading relevant to investigating the issue of equal opportunities in the USA.

For example:

The following receive 1 mark

- Do people have equal opportunities in the USA?
- What barriers exist in the USA?

The following receive 2 marks

- What barriers exist in the USA to women/ethnic minorities achieving equal rights?
- The problems Hispanic Americans face in education in the USA
- How is the law to be used to help women/ethnic minorities achieve equal opportunities in the USA?

(ii) Candidates are required to justify the use of a given method of enquiry.

"Good points" include:

Structured letter—Embassy could provide up to date information, official representative of USA government in UK, have resources to provide information on topic, able to send statistics etc

(iii) Candidates are required to give **two** questions appropriate to investigating the issue of equal opportunities in the USA.

Credit questions which refer to:

- gender
- ethnic origin
- education
- employment
- pay
- family issues
- politics

B—RUSSIA

3. (a) The concept being assessed is **Participation**. Candidates are required to provide detailed explanations.

"Good points" include:

Election for President

Election to Duma

Election to Republic, region, district, cities of St Petersburg and Moscow

(b) The concept being assessed is **Ideology**. Candidates are required to provide detailed explanations.

"Good points" include:

End of communism allows media more freedom to criticise

Free speech is important in a democracy

Need to control actions of government

Wish to avoid the control of the past, censorship etc

(c) (i) Candidates are required to state one aim/heading relevant to investigating the issue of equal opportunities in Russia.

For example:

The following receive 1 mark

- Do people have equal opportunities in Russia?
- Can everyone in Russia have the same chances?

The following receive 2 marks

- Do men and women in Russia have the same opportunity to succeed in politics?
- Do former members of the Communist Party still have more opportunities to succeed in business/politics?
- Do Russians from outside European Russia have the same opportunities?

(ii) Candidates are required to justify the use of a given method of enquiry.

"Good points" include:

- Embassy could provide up to date information
- Official representative of Russia in the UK, so should have information on topic
- Much faster than writing to Russia and would get reply in English
- Any other relevant point

(iii) Candidates are required to give two questions appropriate to investigating the issue of equal opportunities in Russia.

B 3. (c) (iii) continued

Credit questions which refer to:

- gender
- different regions
- education
- employment
- politics
- pay

C—CHINA

3. (a) Candidates are required to provide detailed explanations. The concept being assessed is **Participation**.

"Good points" include:

- the Communist Party is the main political party in China and controls China
- membership of the Communist Party is limited to some Chinese only
- other political parties are controlled by the Communist Party
- elections are carefully controlled by the Communist Party
- political protests and demonstrations are often crushed
- any other relevant point

(b) Candidates are required to provide detailed explanations. The concept being assessed is **Ideology**.

"Good points" include:

- it would allow free speech in China
- opposition to government policy could be shown
- access to world news and views of China would be available
- access to the Internet would allow new ideas into China
- any other valid point

(c) (i) Candidates are required to state one aim/heading relevant to investigating the issue of equal opportunities in China.

For example:

the following receive **one mark**

- Do people have equal opportunities in China?
- What barriers exist in China?

the following receive **two marks**

- How are boys and girls treated in China?
- What barriers exist in China to women achieving equal rights?
- The problems migrants face in getting work in China
- Help given to get equal opportunities for women

C 3. (c) (ii) Candidates are required to justify the use of a given method of enquiry.

Expect reference to:

- Embassy could provide up to date information, pamphlets, statistics etc
- You can get back good answers to your main questions
- They might tell you where to get more information on your topic

(iii) Candidates are required to give two relevant questions appropriate to investigating the issue of equal opportunities in China.

Expect questions which refer to:

- Gender
- Rural/Urban differences
- boys/girls
- education
- industry
- family issues etc

4. (a) The skill being assessed is the ability of candidates to support a given point of view.

"Good points" include:

- agriculture takes almost half (46%) of the total EU spending
- agriculture is by far the largest part of the EU budget, 11% more than next largest item
- the cost of agriculture has risen from 34,000 million ecus in 1993 to 43,100 million ecus in 1999

(b) The concept being assessed is **Need**. Candidates are required to provide detailed explanations.

"Good points" include:

- member countries can receive regional aid
- member countries have more trading partners
- citizens of member countries can work in any EU country
- citizens of member countries have freedom of movement within the EU
- member countries can receive international support from the EU in crises
- any other valid point

(c) The skill being assessed is the ability to make comparisons and draw conclusions.

"Good points" include:

- USSR is no longer an enemy therefore there is a large reduction in force numbers etc
- terrorism is still a threat therefore there is increased training for special forces etc

Modern Studies
General Level
1999 (cont.)

4. (c) continued

- Russia has scrapped nuclear and other weapons so NATO has reduced nuclear missiles etc
- NATO forces may have to operate outwith Europe therefore need for carriers and landing craft
- Peacekeeping role eg Bosnia therefore need for rapid reaction forces

(d)   The concept being assessed is **Power**. Candidates are required to provide detailed explanations.

"Good points" include:

- security from attack
- improved co-operation with former enemies therefore reduced chance of conflict
- reduced overall defence costs because shared amongst more members
- increased military strength and international influence
- any other valid point

Modern Studies
General Level
2000

1. (a)   The concept being assessed is **Representation**. Detailed descriptions are required.

Good points include:

- They can help members fight against unfair treatment in the workplace.
- Trade Unions can help improve wages and conditions.
- Trade Unions can help ensure a healthy workplace.
- They can provide legal assistance and advice to members on a range of issues from Unfair dismissal to Racial/Sexual discrimination to Maternity benefits and Pensions.
- Any other valid point.

(b)   The skill being assessed is the ability to detect exaggeration and provide explanations.

Good points include:

- Unison has many more members than the Musicians Union (MU).
- Unison is dominated by women members whilst men dominate the MU.
- Unison membership is drawn from lots of different trades and industries whilst the MU draws its members solely from within the music industry.
- Any other valid point, based on the Sources.

1. (c)   The concept being assessed is Rights & Responsibilities. Detailed descriptions are required.

Good points include:

- People have the right to demonstrate.
- They have the right to write letters to the Council, Councillor or MP.
- They must not involve themselves in any illegal activity such as climbing into trees to stop them being chopped down or chaining themselves to contractors' machinery. In both cases, they are liable to be arrested by the police.
- Any other valid point.

(d)   The skill being assessed is the ability to make comparisons between sources and draw conclusions.

Good points include:

- The biggest change came with more people finding agreement with party policies. There was an 8% change.
- Voters were more positive in that they were less inclined to vote for a party because their strongest feelings were negative towards other parties. A 7% drop.
- Importance of local candidate has gone down.
- Number of people who vote for a party because they usually support that party has remained constant.
- Any other valid point, based on the Sources.

2. (a)   The concept being assessed is **Ideology**. Detailed descriptions are required.

High marks given for references to specific Labour policies such as New Deal and National Minimum Wage.

Good points include:

- New Deal –

    Full time training and education

    Employment with training

    Environment task force

    Voluntary sector.

All designed to get people back into work immediately or provide them with the skills to get a job. Credit is given for mention of compulsory element.

- Job Seekers Allowance (JSA) and other benefits for unemployed
- Job Centres/Job clubs
- Introduction of National Minimum Wage
- Family Credit and other benefits for those on low incomes
- Any other valid point.

2.(*b*) The concept being assessed is **Equality**. Explanations are required.

Good points include:

- Disabled –

Prejudice and discrimination

Physical problems in being able to do particular jobs

Costs to employers of adapting workplace eg special toilets, lifts

Any other valid point.

- Members of ethnic minorities –

Prejudice and discrimination

Poor educational attainment of some groups

Possible difficulties with language for some groups

Any other valid point.

- Older workers –

Prejudice and discrimination

Need for higher wages

Out of date skills

Fears on health and fitness

Any other valid point.

(*c*) Answers are required to include one aim/heading relevant to investigating the issue of living standards for different types of families.

Credit is given for a variety of styles and responses.

For example:

The following receive 1 mark

- Do all families have the same standard of living?

- Families are not equal.

The following receive 2 marks

- All families do not have the same type of housing.

- Do families have access to the same leisure activities?

(*d*) Answers are required to include justification of the use of a given method of enquiry.

Good points include:

- Able to prepare questions in advance.

- Able to adapt and add extra questions during interview.

- Interviewing an expert in the problem of families who would be able to provide statistics etc to help with the investigation.

- Any other valid point.

(*e*) Answers are required to include two questions appropriate to investigating the issue of living standards for different types of family.

2. (*e*) continued

Credit is given for questions which refer to:

- housing
- leisure
- income
- education
- gender
- any other relevant aspect of living standards.

A – THE USA

3. (*a*) The concept being assessed is **Participation**. Descriptions are required.

Good points include:

- individual making contact with their elected representative or government

- can lobby and campaign against the government

- joining a variety of political movements or interest groups

- standing for election at local, state, federal or Presidential level

- any other valid point.

(*b*) The skill being assessed is the ability to express support for a personal or given point of view with a number of valid, detailed reasons.

Good points include:

- young black women experience more discrimination shopping than older black women, but only 29% to 28%

- young black women experience substantially more discrimination eating out than older black women, 28% to 16%

- shopping and eating out are the areas of highest discrimination and young black women experience the worst discrimination in these areas

- any other valid point, based on the Sources.

(*c*) The concept being assessed is **Equality**. Explanations are required.

Good points include:

- America being the land of opportunity for all but only some do well.

- Housing, education and health standards are very high in the USA for some.

- Some Americans work hard and achieve the American Dream of wealth and prosperity.

- Some Americans can get access to better school and college education and so help their employment prospects.

- Some Americans are able to own and run their own business.

- Some Americans do not face prejudice and discrimination.

- Any other valid point.

Modern Studies
General Level
2000 (cont.)

A 3. (d) The skill being assessed is the ability to detect and explain examples of lack of objectivity in straightforward sources.

Good points include:

- **Source 1** says Democrats want to "make sure the American Dream is available to all" while **Source 2** says Republicans want to "increase the number Americans achieving the American Dream". **These are similar policies on the American Dream**.

- **Source 1** says Democrats want "a strong foreign policy to keep America as a powerful country", while **Source 2** says Republicans want to "keep America's position as one of the most powerful countries in the world". These are similar policies on America and world power.

- any other valid point, based on the Sources.

B – RUSSIA

3. (a) The concept being assessed is **Participation**. Descriptions are required.

Good points include:

- Wide variety of political movements to join.
- Freedom to organise and set up political movements.
- Right to stand for election.
- Right to lobby and campaign against the government.
- Any other valid points.

(b) The skill being assessed is the ability to express support for a personal or given point of view with a number of valid, detailed reasons.

Good points include:

- Women are more likely to be unemployed than men in Russia—65% compared to 38%.
- The number of women in the Duma is far less than men—9% compared to 91%.
- In Novolski, 75% of the unemployed are women.
- Any other valid points, based on the Sources.

B 3. (c) The concept being assessed is **Equality**. Explanations are required.

Good points include:

- Some people have set up their own businesses.
- Some workers earn high wages and bonuses, especially if working for foreign firms.
- Some workers have shares in private enterprises.
- Unemployment is rising faster in some regions than others
- Inflation has wiped out savings
- State employees and pensioners are poor—some people have not been paid for months
- Food prices have risen sharply
- Credit any other valid point.

(d) The skill being assessed is the ability to detect and explain examples of lack of objectivity in straightforward sources.

Good points include:

- Communists wish to improve the living standards of the Russian people. Liberal Democrats wish to improve the economy and living standards.
- Communists wish to govern Russia through democratic methods. Liberal Democrats wish to improve democracy throughout Russia.
- Any other valid point, based on the Sources.

C – CHINA

3. (a) The concept being assessed is **Participation**. Descriptions are required.

Good points include:

- Participation in workplace decision-making groups
- Joining the Communist Party
- Participating in other political groups, including those expressing dissent
- Attending meetings of political groups
- Participation in neighbourhood committees/groups
- Any other valid point.

(b) The skill being assessed is the ability to express support for a personal or given point of view with a number of valid, detailed reasons.

Good points include:

- More men than women are employed in coal mining (95% as opposed to 5%).
- More men than women are employed in the police (75% as opposed to 25%).
- Any other valid point, based on the Sources.

C 3. (c) The concept being assessed is **Equality**. Explanations are required.

Good points include:

- Some people live in areas that have seen faster economic growth, giving them a great chance of good standard of living.
- Rural-urban disparities.
- People employed by foreign companies generally earn higher incomes than those working for Chinese businesses.
- Privileged elites within the Communist Party and the political machinery have higher living standards.
- Any other valid point.

(d) The skill being assessed is the ability to detect and explain examples of lack of objectivity in straightforward sources.

Good points include:

- Both groups support the idea that Macau should be handed back to Chinese government, in the same way as Hong Kong was.
- Both groups believe that the environment should receive more attention than it has in the past.
- Any other valid point, based on the Sources.

4. (a) The skill being assessed is the ability to detect exaggeration and provide valid explanations.

The exaggerated sentences are:

- All four African countries have seen a reduction in the percentage of their national income that comes from aid.
- In Kenya the percentage of national income coming from aid has remained the same.

These two sentences must then be linked to an appropriate explanation. These are given below.

- Not all countries have seen a reduction in the percentage of national income that comes from aid—Chad has seen an increase.
- In Kenya the percentage of national income coming from aid has not remained the same—it has almost halved.

(b) The skill being assessed is the ability to make comparisons within a source and draw conclusions.

Accept reference to:

- For Cameroon

    Percentage of population with access to safe water is less

    Percentage of national wealth spent on health is lower

4. (b) continued

- For Cote d'Ivoire

    Higher rate of infant deaths

    More children suffering from malnutrition

- Any any other valid point, based on the Sources.

(c) The concept being assessed is **Need**. Descriptions are required.

Accept reference to any relevant examples of small-scale aid projects, such as:

- Water supplies
- Irrigation
- Hill slope terracing
- Local medical centres
- Any other valid points.

(d) The skill being assessed is the ability to support and oppose a given view.

Credit is given for reference to:

Support the view:

- Other countries have sold weapons to rebels in Sierra Leone (Source 2)

Oppose the view:

- The division between the two groups in Sierra Leone has caused the war (Source 1)

Any other valid point, based on the Sources.

Modern Studies General Level 2001

1. (a) The concept being assessed is **Representation**. Detailed descriptions are required.

Good points include:

- By holding surgeries in their constituencies they can hear about individual issues and problems
- They can write letters on behalf of their constituents
- They can raise points in debates in the Parliament
- They can ask questions to Ministers in the Parliament
- They can vote in Parliament according to the views of their constituents
- Any other valid point.

(b) The skill being assessed is the ability to make comparisons within a source and draw conclusions.

- The support of the Labour Party fell considerably from 38% to 22% in a 10 month period
- Support for the Conservative Party held up well and they won the seat at the by-election

Modern Studies
General Level
2001 (cont.)

1. (b) continued

- Support for the SNP increased by 10% and they pushed the Labour Party into third place at the by-election
- Any other valid point, based on the Sources

(c) Answers are required to include two aims/headings relevant to investigating the issue of methods used by members of a Pressure Group during a campaign to improve road safety.

The following would receive 1 mark:

- To find out the different types of methods used by members of this pressure group
- To find out which method appears most successful and which appears least successful
- Any other valid point.

(d) Answers are required to include justification of the use of a given method of enquiry.

- You can work out exactly what you want to ask beforehand
- You can ensure that it is the most appropriate person who is answering your questions
- Any other valid point.

(e) Answers are required to include two questions appropriate to investigating the issue of methods used by members of a Pressure Group during a campaign to improve road safety.

The following questions would be awarded two marks each.

- Which of the following methods have you used in your campaign?

  a) leafleting

  b) letters to local newspaper

  c) letter to Councillor

  d) demonstration

  e) any other (please state)

- Which method appeared to get the biggest response from the public?

The following questions would be awarded one mark each:

- Have you used lots of different methods?   Yes/No
- Do some methods work better than others?   Yes/No

2. (a) The concept being assessed is **Need**. Detailed descriptions are required.

Good points include:

- Able to call warden or helpline in an emergency
- Adaptations to meet the needs of elderly people, eg bathroom door opening outwards, waist level power sockets etc
- Central heating
- Social aspects—eg coffee mornings, communal lounge, organised outings, bingo
- Protection but with the ability to retain independence
- Any other valid point.

(b) The skill being assessed is the ability to detect exaggeration and provide explanations.

Both sources must be used for full marks.

Source 1—linked to sentence 2 of the view

- In no age group are there more men than women
- Amongst the over 80s there are three times as many women
- Between 75 and 84 years only one-third are men
- Between 60 and 74 years there is a difference of 18% between men and women

Source 2—linked to sentence 3 of the view

- Much higher percentage of Black Caribbean
- Percentage figure varies from 3% to 12%
- Each group has a different level of percentage that are elderly
- Any other valid point, from the Sources.

(c) The concept being assessed is **Equality**. Explanations are required.

Good points include:

- Private pensions and insurance schemes give a higher living standard than existing on the state Old Age Pension
- Savings and inheritance factors
- Differences in employment and wage levels
- Number of children in the family
- Differences in the cost of living depending on the area people live in
- Any other valid point.

2. (*d*) The skill being assessed is the ability to provide support for a given point of view.

Good points include:

- Drop of 10% in average income of poorest families compared to average overall rise of 44%
- UK has the highest percentage of children living in poverty (32%)
- Any other point

A – THE USA

3. (*a*) The concept being assessed is **Participation**. Detailed descriptions are required.

A USA example must be given for full marks.

Good points include:

- Contact their elected representative or a government body about the issue
- Join an interest group to lobby, campaign and protest to try and influence the government
- Contact the media about a problem or issue
- Stand for election themselves with their own ideas on issues
- Any other valid point.

(*b*) The skill being assessed is the ability to make comparisons between sources and draw conclusions.

- Source 1 says "The USA has a good human rights record" BUT Source 2 says that "The human rights record of the USA is terrible."
- Source 1 says "The death penalty is a good punishment for . . . serious crime" BUT Source 2 says that "The death penalty is wrong for any crime."
- Source 1 says "It is the right of American people to own guns" BUT Source 2 says that "The USA must stop young people from having the right to own guns."
- Any other valid point, from the Sources.

(*c*) The concept being assessed is **Ideology**. Explanations are required.

A USA example must be given for full marks.

Good points include:

- The USA is one of the richest countries in the world per head of population
- Unemployment is very low
- If you work hard then you can become rich and successful, and possibly even own your own company—the American Dream
- Education, housing, health standards etc are very good
- Any other valid point.

A 3. (*d*) The skill being assessed is the ability to detect exaggeration and provide explanations.

Good points include:

Source 1

- The number of blacks in the House of Representatives has risen from 17 in 1980 to 38 in 2000—this is an improvement

Source 2

- Various choices that show improvement—black employment and home ownership increasing, percentage of blacks below poverty line decreasing, percentage of black elected officials is the highest ever
- Any other valid point, from the Sources.

B – RUSSIA

3. (*a*) The concept being assessed is **Participation**. Detailed descriptions are required.

A Russian example must be given for full marks.

Good points include:

- Lots of political/protest movements to join
- Ability to join a political party and be involved in its policy making
- Participant in campaigns/lobby
- Taking part in strikes/demonstrations
- Any other valid point.

(*b*) The skill being assessed is the ability to make comparisons between sources and draw conclusions.

Good points include:

- Source 1 says that the world "has a responsibility" BUT Source 2 states "outsiders should not try to interfere."
- Source 1 claims innocent Chechens were killed or injured by the Russian Army BUT Source 2 says only terrorists have been killed, not ordinary people.
- Any other valid point, from the Sources.

(*c*) The concept being assessed is **Ideology**. Explanations are required.

A Russian example must be given for full marks.

Good points include:

- Unfair—people working for foreign businesses are advantaged
- Unemployment is rising faster in some areas than in others
- Rapid inflation has wiped out the value of savings
- Some state workers (eg coal miners, members of the armed forces) may not have been paid for months
- Any other valid point.

Modern Studies
General Level
2001 (cont.)

B 3. (d) The skill being assessed is the ability to detect exaggeration and provide explanations.

Good points include:

- Martinov states "support remained constant" however Source 1 shows it ranged from 35% to 53%
- Martinov also claims both parties were delighted with the outcome of the Duma elections but they both got virtually the same number of seats and were beaten by "others"
- Any other valid point, from the Sources.

C – CHINA

3. (a) The concept being assessed is **Participation**. Detailed descriptions are required.

A Chinese example must be given for full marks.

Good points include:

- Joining the Communist Party
- Participating in other political groups, including those expressing dissent
- Attending meetings of political groups
- Participation in neighbourhood/ workplace committees
- Any other valid point.

(b) The skill being assessed is the ability to make comparisons between sources and draw conclusions.

Good points include:

- Source 1 says that the religious freedom of citizens is protected but Source 2 says that members of religious groups have been arrested
- Source 1 says all citizens enjoy human rights but Source 2 says that many people are unhappy with the government because they are not given human rights
- Any other valid point, from the Sources.

(c) The concept being assessed is **Ideology**. Explanations are required.

A Chinese example must be given for full marks.

Good points include:

- Economic boom in recent years
- Private businesses allow increased wealth for some
- Special Economic Zones have attracted foreign investment and have become growth areas
- Responsibility System has allowed some farmers to increase their wealth
- Any other valid points

C 3. (d) The skill being assessed is the ability to detect exaggeration and provide explanations.

Good points include:

- Ho Hun Yan says that ordinary citizens get few opportunities to vote, Source 1 says they can vote at village, workplace, provincial and national level
- Ho Hun Yan says that the turnout at elections is low, but Source 2 shows turnout to be over 90%
- Any other valid point from the Sources.

4. (a) The concept being assessed is **Power**. Detailed descriptions are required.

Answers may refer to NATO, the United Nations or both.

Good points include:

NATO

- Military intervention to end conflicts in Bosnia and Kosovo
- Bombing of Serbian targets

United Nations

- Economic sanctions against Serbia
- Peacekeeping forces (eg KFOR)
- Humanitarian aid for refugees
- Any other valid point.

(b) The skill being assessed is the ability to provide support and opposition for a given point of view.

Good points include:

SUPPORT

- Over half of the people surveyed in Central Scotland are in favour of Britain joining the Single European Currency before 2005—the first bar graph confirms this through the proportions for "immediately" and "within three years"

OPPOSE

- People also believe that the European Union should have more powers—the second bar graph does not bear this out. The largest group of people do not think the EU should have more powers.
- Any other valid point from the Sources.

(c) The concept being assessed is **Need**. Explanations are required.

Good points include:

- Financial support for disadvantaged areas through the Regional/Social Policies
- Subsidies for farmers through the Common Agricultural Policy
- Provides Scottish businesses with access to the European market
- Gives Scottish people the opportunity to live, study and work in Europe
- Any other valid point

4. (*d*) The skill being assessed is the ability to make comparisons within a source and draw conclusions.

Points which simply repeat figures from the table without comment gain zero marks. Points that make minimal comparison should be awarded one mark.

Points worthy of two marks include:

- Three countries have seen a decline and one has seen an increase
- Total number of troops has declined
- Biggest country has seen a major decline in the number of troops
- The number of Turkish troops has risen from 800 to 820 thousand

The points below give further illustration of 1 and 2 mark points:

- The number of UK troops has gone down slightly—2 mark point
- The number of Turkish troops has gone up—1 mark point
- The number of American troops has gone down—1 mark point
- The number of German troops has gone down slightly—2 mark point

Modern Studies
General Level
2002

1. (*a*) The concept being assessed is **Participation**. Candidates are required to provide detailed descriptions.

"Good points" include:

- Becoming a shop steward
- Attending union meetings
- Voting at elections for various posts
- Taking part in industrial action
- Any other valid point

(*b*) Candidates are required to make comparisons within and between sources and draw conclusions.

"Good points" include:

- Difference 1—72% of UNISON is female compared to only 26% of TGWU
- Difference 2—More women are taking positions of responsibility in UNISON but not many in the TGWU have become union officials
- Any other valid point

(*c*) The concept being assessed is **Rights and Responsibilities**. Candidates are requried to provide detailed explanations.

"Good points" include:

- Voting is a responsibility in a democracy, so people should use their right to elect representatives

1. (*c*) continued

- People who do not vote do not have the right to complain about election results or decisions taken by elected representatives
- Election results based on low turnouts are less reliable—there is widespread concern about the lowering of turnout in most democratic countries
- Any other valid point

(*d*) Candidates are required to provide support for a given point of view.

Source 2 linked to:

- Some councils will improve their services because they are planning to spend more on social work and education

Source 1 linked to:

- Cities will pay more as Edinburgh and Glasgow pay far more than Scottish Borders and the Western Isles
- Any other valid point

2. (*a*) Candidates are required to detect exaggeration and provide explanations.

Link to Source 1:

- Unemployment in Scotland increasing. This part of the view is exaggerated because the table shows that unemployment in Scotland has fallen between 1998 and 1999

Link to Source 2:

- The Netherlands, Sweden and Portugal all have lower unemployment than the UK. This part of the view is exaggerated because Sweden has higher unemployment than the UK

(*b*) The concept being assessed is **Need**. Candidates are required to provide detailed descriptions.

"Good points" include:

- By providing benefits so that they can buy items that they require
- By paying Housing Benefit so that they have accommodation to live in
- By providing training schemes to try and give them the skills and experience necessary to find a job
- By trying to attract business to the UK to create more jobs
- Any other valid point

(*c*) The concept being assessed is **Equality**. Candidates are required to provide explanations.

"Good points" include:

- Differences in employment status and wage levels
- Problems faced by some lone parent families
- Number of children in the family
- Financial problems caused by addiction
- Any other valid point

Modern Studies
General Level
2002 (cont.)

2. (d) Candidates are required to make comparisons within a source and draw conclusions.

- Single pensioners get a lot more of their income from benefits (63%) than other households
- Households with two adults and or children get more income from wages than other groups
- Single pensioners have the lowest percentage of income from wages at only 3%
- Any other valid point

A—THE USA

3. (a) The concept being assessed is **Equality**. Candidates are required to provide detailed descriptions.

"Good points" include:

Housing

- Blacks and Hispanics are more likely than Whites to live in poorer housing
- The majority of urban Blacks and Hispanics live in ghettos in the inner city
- Blacks have a higher percentage of single parent families headed by women than Whites
- Blacks and Hispanics are less likely to own houses
- Any other valid point

Health

- Black and Hispanic health statistics are likely to be worse than Whites
- Blacks, Hispanics and Native Americans are less likely to have health insurance than Whites
- Black infant mortality is about double that of Whites
- Blacks have a higher percentage of AIDS sufferers and deaths than Whites
- Any other valid point

Crime and Justice

- Black and Hispanic crime statistics are likely to be worse than whites
- Nearly half of all murder victims in the USA are black
- Blacks and Hispanics feel that they face more prejudice and discrimination from the police and courts, eg Rodney King case
- Black and Hispanics are more likely than Whites to be in jail
- Any other valid point

(b) The concept being assessed is **Ideology**. Candidates are required to provide detailed explanations.

A 3. (b) continued

"Good points" include:

- If you do well at school, college or university (eg Harvard) you can achieve good qualifications and get a well-paid job
- If you work hard in the USA you could achieve the American Dream by owning your own business and making a lot of money, eg Bill Gates and Microsoft—some young Americans make millions by starting up their own companies
- The USA is one of the richest countries in the world so people have a better chance of becoming rich, eg Bill Gates
- Any other valid point

(c) Candidates are required to provide support and opposition for a given point of view.

"Good points" include:

- Support

Eva Kaye said "Most men are happy with the result of the 2000 Presidential Election in the USA". Source 2 shows that 53% of men voted for Bush. This supports Eva's view as most men are happy that Bush won

- Oppose

Eva Kaye said "The person with the most Popular Votes became President". Source 1 shows that Bush, who became President, had 50·4 million popular votes while Gore had 50·9 million popular votes—more than Bush. This opposes Eva's view, as the person with most popular votes did not become President

- Any other valid point

(d) Candidates are required to detect exaggeration and provide explanations.

"Good points" include:

Reason 1

Jay Schulz said "The School Voucher Programme will benefit all pupils"

Source 1 says that "The School Voucher Programme will hurt poor ethnic minority communities." This shows that Jay Schulz was exaggerating, as it will not help all pupils

OR

Source 1 says that "The School Voucher Programme . . . will leave government-run schools with even fewer resources and funds and cause even more problems for ethnic minorities." This shows that Jay Schulz was exaggerating because it will not help all pupils

Reason 2

Jay Schulz said "Government-run schools do not have modern facilities like access to the internet"

Source 2 shows that 97% of government-run schools were on the Internet in 2000. This shows that Jay Schulz was exaggerating as they have modern facilities

B—RUSSIA

3. (a) The concept being assessed is **Equality**. Candidates are required to provide detailed descriptions.

Candidates may deal with "unfair treatment" in any context—economic, social or political.

Credit reference to migrant groups living within Russia.

"Good points" include:

- Repression of nationalist minorities in areas such as Chechnya
- Exploitation of economic migrants
- Xenophobia towards foreign workers/migrants
- Social disadvantage faced by rural population
- Any other valid point

(b) The concept being assessed is **Ideology**. Candidates are required to provide detailed explanations.

"Good points" include:

- Earns valuable foreign currency
- Provides employment opportunities—often at better wage rates than local businesses can pay
- Improves living standards for local people by extending consumer choice
- May make government more popular because they are seen to be improving living conditions
- Any other valid point

(c) Candidates are required to provide support and opposition for a given point of view.

"Good points" include:

- Support

  Yevgeny Lovchev says that "Vladimir Putin was a clear winner" in the 2000 Presidential Election. Source 2 shows that Putin gained 53% of the vote which gave him victory by an overall majority. This supports the view of Lovchev

- Oppose

  Yevgeny Lovchev says that "One party has an overall majority in the Duma". Source 1 shows that this is not true as there is no overall majority in the Duma. This opposes the view of Lovchev

- Any other valid point

(d) Candidates are required to detect exaggeration and provide explanations.

Reason 1

Boris Demianenko says that "the construction industry has seen an increase in importance". This is exaggerated because Source 1 shows that the importance of the construction industry has declined between 1900 and 1998

B 3. (d) continued

Reason 2

Boris Demianenko said "all Russian workers are now paid on a regular basis". This is exaggerated because Source 2 shows that coal miners in the Vorkuta basin have not been paid on a regular basis for several months now

C—CHINA

3. (a) The concept being assessed is **Equality**. Candidates are required to provide detailed descriptions.

"Good points" include:

- Rural population feel that they do not enjoy the same economic advantages as people in the cities
- Urban population feel that they do not enjoy the same political freedoms as people in villages
- Differences in economic situation between designated Special Economic Zones and other areas
- Differences in economic situation between Hong Kong and other areas
- Repression of nationalist groups in Tibet

(b) The concept being assessed is **Ideology**. Candidates are required to provide detailed explanations.

"Good points" include:

- Earns valuable foreign currency
- Helps to attract tourists to China
- Provides employment opportunities—often at better wage rates than local businesses can pay
- Improves living standards for local people by extending consumer choice
- May make government more popular because they are seen to be improving living conditions
- Any other valid point

(c) Candidates are required to provide support and opposition for a given point of view.

"Good points" include:

- Support

  Fan Zhiyi said that the Communist Party was the largest political party in China. Source 1 supports this because the Communist Party has by far and away the largest membership of any political organisation

- Oppose

  Fan Zhiyi said that all members of the party agree on future policies. Source 2 opposes this—it says that some members want to make the party more modern and some want no change to hard-line policies

- Any other valid point

Modern Studies
General Level
2002 (cont.)

C 3. (*d*)   Candidates are required to detect exaggeration and provide explanations.

Reason 1

Wan Zee says the Chinese are correct to blame America for this incident. Source 1 says that "Investigation reveals that the Chinese jet rammed the spy plane causing it to crash land . . ."

Reason 2

Wan Zee says that China is happy about American links with Taiwan. Source 2 shows China is unhappy about the US selling weapons to Taiwan

4. (*a*)   The concept being assessed is **Need**. Candidates are required to provide detailed descriptions.

"Good points" include:

- Aid agencies such as FAO, WHO or UNICEF can help greatly
- FAO can provide expertise to ensure that crops grow as well as possible
- Experts give advice on how to get the maximum from resources that are available
- WHO can organise immunisation programmes
- Set-up small-scale health centres or train people to be doctors or nurses
- They can also provide food aid through the World Food Programme
- Can also meet the needs of refugees through the work of UNHCR
- Peace-keeping forces to maintain stability in war zones
- Any other valid point

(*b*)   Candidates are required to make comparisons within a source.

"Good points" include:

- Ethiopia has the smallest average income per head and also the fewest adults who can read and write. Life expectancy at 45 is also the lowest of the 4 countries
- Gabon has the highest average income but it does not mean that they would have the biggest percentage of adults who can read and write. At 63% this is still 15% below the figure of Kenya
- Although Sudan's population has the second lowest income, its people live longer (57 years) than people from any of the other countries
- Any other valid point

4. (*c*)   Candidates are required to give relevant aims/headings for an investigation topic.

The following receive 1 mark:

- To find out the different types of aid which the UK gives to developing countries in Africa
- To find out how successful the aid has been in various African countries

(*d*)   Candidates are required to give advantages/disadvantages of a given method of enquiry

Advantages

- He is the Minister so he should have all the information required
- You can take time to frame questions to get the maximum amount of information

Disadvantages

- The only information you get is what you ask for—there is no follow-up
- You have no guarantee that you will get a reply from a government Minister

(*e*)   Candidates are required to demonstrate the ability to use a given method of enquiry.

- How much does the UK give in the form of aid to developing countries in Africa?
- Which countries in Africa does the UK give aid to?
- How do you decide who should get the aid from the UK?

Modern Studies
Credit Level
1998

1. (*a*)   The candidate is required to make comparisons within and between complex sources and draw valid **conclusions**.

"Good points" include:

- 3% more voted for Labour in Scotland than they did in the UK as a whole
- 46% of the votes cast in Scotland got Labour approximately 70% of the seats available
- Although getting less than half the votes cast, Labour achieved a huge electoral victory with an overall majority of 179
- Support for Labour was strongest in the North of England where they achieved over 50% of the popular vote
- In South West England, they came third in terms of the popular vote behind the Conservatives and the Conservatives also had the biggest share of the vote in South East England
- Labour did massively well amongst first time voters. 57% as opposed to 19% for the Conservatives
- Labour lagged behind the Conservatives amongst elderly voters

1. (a) continued

- Labour did well amongst traditional supporters eg Council tenants and trade union members with more than 50% of each voting for them
- Labour got the biggest percentage of the votes cast (41%) amongst what was traditionally reckoned to be Conservative voters, namely the Homeowners
- The view that the Conservatives tend to attract more female votes than labour was not true in 1997
- Any other valid point.

(b) The concept being assessed is **Rights & Responsibilities**. Candidates are expected to use their understanding of the concept to provide explanations in depth and detail.

Credit discussion of the effects of not accepting responsibilities eg by breaking the law.

"Good points" include:

- Newspapers have the freedom to report the news freely
- Newspapers are able to put their own interpretation on the news and show potential bias
- They can publish Opinion Polls and other information which make impact on the government
- They have a responsibility to ensure that they do not libel any person or party, publish inaccurate information etc
- Pressure groups have the right to attempt to get their message across in any way shape or form so long as it is within the law
- Rights include assembly, public demonstrations, lobbying elected representatives, use of the media and other publicity, canvassing public support, using professional lobbyists etc
- Responsibilities include staying within the law, not falsifying/exaggerating claims etc
- Any other valid point.

(c) The concept being assessed is **Representation**. Candidates are expected to use their understanding of the concept to provide explanations in depth and detail.

Credit reference to specific forms of PR but note the question does not demand this.

"Good points" include:

Against PR (in favour of FPTP)

- Straightforward
- Easy to understand
- People can relate to local MP who wins the election in a particular constituency
- Little chance of extremist parties winning any seats usually gives a clear majority in House of Commons so avoiding coalitions

1. (c) continued

For:

- Far too many "wasted" votes under FPTP
- % of votes corresponding with the number of MPs is much fairer with PR
- Most European countries do not use FPTP
- Fairer to smaller parties especially "middle of the road" eg Lib Dems
- More women, ethnic minorities likely to be elected under some PR systems
- Governments no longer able to railroad controversial measures through parliament with under 50% of popular vote

2. (a) The candidate is required to make comparisons within and between complex sources and draw valid conclusions.

"Good points" include:

Option A—Sheltered Housing

- Visitors bedrooms available—none of her relatives live closer than 75 miles away
- Alarm system to contact warden—may be sensible after she slipped and broke her leg last winter
- Communal lounge available—she may be lonely, her husband having died

Option B—Private Nursing Home

- Lounge facilities shared—she may be lonely, her husband having died
- Regular visiting opportunities for families and friends
- Special menus available—to suit her dietary needs
- 24 hour care available—she is becoming slightly forgetful

Reasons for rejecting each option:

Option A—Sheltered Housing

- Broke leg last winter; forgetful—Mrs Wilkie appears to need round-the-clock care
- Forgetful/special dietary requirements—in Sheltered Housing she would be responsible for cooking her own meals

Option B—Nursing Home

- May not want to share a bedroom with anyone else
- All meals cooked and cleaning done—loss of independence
- Any other valid point should be credited.

Award a maximum of 4 marks when only reasons for the choice are given. The additional 2 marks are available for candidates who explain why they have rejected the other option.

Modern Studies
Credit Level
1998 (cont.)

2. (b) The candidate is required to explain instances of the selective use of facts, giving developed arguments.

"Good points" include:

- Source 1—As a person gets older their ability to carry out various activities declines. Expect figures to be quoted for at least one of the activities.
- Source 2—Former male professionals are less likely than other groups to report long-standing illness— 49% as opposed to 60% + in all other categories.

(c) The concept being assessed is **Need**. Candidates are expected to use their understanding of the concept to provide explanations in depth and detail.

"Good points" include:

- Alterations to housing to meet the health needs of elderly people (eg stair lifts, grab rails, panic buttons etc). These factors should be grouped together into one point, and awarded a maximum of three marks
- Hip replacement operations to improve mobility
- Pacemakers
- Any other valid point.

(d) The concept being assessed is **Ideology**. Candidates are expected to use their understanding of the concept to provide explanations in depth and detail.

"Good points" include:

Single parent families

Support the view:

- Less government help would allow reduction in government spending and reduced taxation
- Single parent families should not be supported by the government—this could lead to less break-up of families and births to single mothers

Oppose the view:

- Some families will receive little or no help, apart from that given by the government
- Less government help to single parent families would penalise people who may already be very poor. The families of single parents may not have the means to support them

The unemployed

Support the view:

- Some unemployed people are happy to "live off the state". Reducing government help would encourage them to find work
- Lower government spending on unemployed people would allow reduced taxation, creating more jobs because business people would have more incentive to expand

2. (d) continued

Oppose the View:

- Many unemployed people have little chance of finding work because of their age, location etc. They are already amongst the poorest people in the country
- Some unemployed people have no families or other sources of support
- The families of unemployed people may not have the means to support them

In each case the points mentioned above are indicative only, and any other valid points are acceptable.

Candidates who do not state a clear view should not be penalised, provided they give a clear justification for their "neutral stance".

ie a candidate providing conflicting reasons should not be penalised if they clearly state that they are undecided about their view.

A—THE USA

3. (a) The concept being assessed is **Ideology**. Candidates are expected to use their understanding of the concept to provide explanations in depth and detail.

"Good points" include:

- private ownership of property and profit motive encourages enterprise and initiative leading to hard work, new ideas, innovation
- competition raises standards, forces firms to compete on quality and price in order to attract and retain customers
- success of economy has resulted in high levels of employment, high wages and high living standards for Americans
- minimum of government interference in running of businesses and low taxes on business encourages the setting up of business and enterprise economy
- Any other valid point.

(b) The concept being assessed is **Equality**. Candidates are expected to explain, in detail, how various factors interact.

"Good points" include:

- poorer housing conditions/ghettos due to lower incomes, reliance on welfare—explanation of poverty cycle
- educational disadvantage/higher dropout rate/poorer qualifications may be caused by lower quality schooling in areas with high concentration of African-Americans and Hispanics, Hispanics may face problems due to language difficulties
- poorer health as exemplified by lower life expectancy, higher infant mortality rates, due to lower level of health insurance cover, lower living standard and poorer housing conditions
- higher incidence of single parents families resulting in lower incomes, higher unemployment and higher incidence of poverty

A 3. (b) continued

- many black and Hispanic Americans face prejudice and discrimination in employment, housing, education, criminal justice system
- public welfare programmes reduced in recent years, cuts in affirmative action programmes etc
- lower registration level amongst African and Hispanic Americans leading to lower turnout in elections, illegal status a bar to many Hispanics voting
- few role models in prominent political positions, never been president or vice president from ethnic minorities
- racial issues given a low priority amongst main parties at the moment
- ethnic minorities may feel alienated from political process due to poor socio-economic position and lack of political representation at most levels of political system
- Any other valid point.

(c) The skill being assessed is the ability of candidates to detect and explain **selective use of facts**.

"Good points" include:

- Source 1 indicates that immigration was an issue in the 1996 Presidential election campaign, both main candidates were concerned about the issue and put forward or backed policies to deal with illegal immigration and President Clinton wishes to see a gradual reduction in legal immigration
- Source 2 indicates that there is no large majority wishing to see immigration made more difficult from any of the places mentioned, in each case less than half wish to make immigration more difficult, in the case of Eastern Europe as many wish to make immigration easier as wish to make it more difficult—39% in both cases
- Source 3 shows that immigration does not have to have a damaging effect on the economy, they come to work and contribute tax revenues of $20 million. Hispanic wages are lower than the Californian average—resulting in lower wage costs for firms. Contribution to agricultural industry
- Any other valid point.

B—RUSSIA

3. (a) The concept being assessed is **Ideology**. Candidates are expected to use their understanding of the concept to provide explanations in depth and detail.

"Good points" include:

- Breakup of the Soviet Union into independent republics
- Removal of Communist Party from role

B 3. (a) continued

- New political parties set up
- Elections to Duma and for President
- Changing role of the media in politics, eg opinion polls, criticism of the government
- Freedoms including to join political parties, to form pressure groups, demonstrating, etc
- Specific events like the attempted coup
- Any other valid point.

(b) The concept being addressed is **Equality**. Candidates are expected to use their understanding of the concept to provide explanations in depth and detail.

"Good points" include:

- Some people are now able to set up their own businesses and can make profits
- Some workers earn higher wages and bonuses, especially if working for foreign firms
- Many workers have shares in privatised state enterprises
- Quality and variety of goods in the shops has improved

But

Unemployment now exists

- Many factories have closed or declined in production
- Many people are poor, especially pensioners and those still employed by the state, eg teachers
- Most cannot afford the goods in the shops as price controls have virtually gone, and supply especially of food can be erratic, eg Mafia control of supply
- Crime has risen greatly, especially petty crime and by children
- Inflation has wiped out savings and created problems for the economy
- Families have been affected by removal of state provision, eg of nurseries
- Any other social problems

(c) The candidate is required to explain instances of **selective use of facts**, giving developed arguments.

Maximum of 6 marks if all sources not used.

"Good points" include:

Source 1

Life in Chechnya is different from that in Russia as they have a different religion. Contrasting views on solution of problems

Source 2

Casualties on both sides have been high, especially on the Chechen side

Source 3

The peace plan shows that all remaining problems are not solved as there has still to be a referendum on full independence. Still violent incidents

Modern Studies
Credit Level
1998 (cont.)

C—CHINA

3. (a) The concept being assessed is **Ideology**. Candidates are required to use understanding of course concepts to provide explanations of the situation in some depth and detail with relevant examples and appropriate generalisations.

"Good points" include:

- the Communist Party represents the people so there is no need for more than one political party

- a one party state—no opposition to the Communist Party is allowed to give the Communist Party total control, "The Party knows best"

- the Communist Party is able to run and control all levels of society from village committees to the national parliament for the good of the country

- local Communist Party officials explain government policy at town and village level which is then implemented by local Committees for the good of the country

- the Communist Party only allows "Freedom within Limits", its own limits and doesn't allow other political parties

- the Communist Party is willing to use the army against dissidents eg Tiananmen Square, to keep its total control

- dissent means that something is wrong and communist ideology cannot be wrong

(b) The concept being assessed is **Equality**. Candidates are required to explain how various factors interact to affect individuals and/or groups.

"Good points" include:

Social Factors

- education and health care are slowly becoming a two tier system with the best for those who can afford it

- there is increasing social division as people have been encouraged to think more about themselves as individuals and not collectively

- those following the One Child Policy are better off as they get preference in education and housing and possible wage bonuses while those that do not follow the policy are financially penalised

- the One Chid Policy means that child deaths for girls are greater than for boys due to girl infanticide etc

- crime is on the increase, especially in the cities, as some migrants are unable to find work

C 3. (b) continued

Economic factors

- the unevenness of economic development throughout China eg better near the coast in Special Economic Zones

- some Chinese are running their own business and so can become very wealthy

- the majority of Chinese continue to live in the countryside where living conditions are poor and so massive inequality between rural and urban areas

- unemployment is rising causing inequality between different groups

- the growth of the Responsibility System in farming means some peasants can choose what and how much they produce and sell the extra produced in private markets

- only those with good farm land have benefited from the agricultural reforms

- some peasants have been able to set up "sideline" business, employ others and keep any profits

- migrants move from rural areas to urban areas, some find better paid work, some do not and become homeless, unemployed, impoverished migrants

(c) Candidates are required to detect and explain examples of lack of objectivity in complex sources, giving developed argument when required. **Selective use of facts**.

"Good points" include:

- the fact that China and Hong Kong are very different socially and have very different populations, countryside populations, literacy and infant mortality (source 1)

- the fact that China and Hong Kong are very different economically and have very different unemployment rates, wealth and consumer good ownership (source 1)

- some young people in Hong Kong were worried that they would have less democracy and worse human rights, more unemployment and increased corruption (source 2)

- the fact that there are some problems as the council, elected in 1995, was abolished (source 3)

- the fact that the Chinese Government is changing the way of life in Hong Kong as it refused to recognise Hong Kong's "Bill of Rights" and promises to respect Human Rights may not be kept

- the Chinese army has moved into Hong Kong

The candidate may also mention that the Chinese politician is saying that Hong Kong and China are similar, everyone in Hong Kong is pleased about being part of China and that there have been no problems as there will be no change in the way of life in Hong Kong

4. (*a*) The concepts being assessed are **Need** and **Power**. Candidates are required to explain in detail how various factors interact.

Credit specific knowledge of East European countries but do not insist on it.

Accept (NATO):

- protection from attack—guarantee of help from other NATO members
- fear of Russia still very real
- USA is the leading superpower and in NATO
- nuclear umbrella
- training opportunities to upgrade forces
- access to modern equipment
- peace keeping role relevant in East Europe

Accept (EU):

- poor living standards in East resulting from backward economies
- access to markets
- access to structural fund to help poor/remote/other disadvantaged regions
- access to CAP particularly attractive to east Europe
- security problems in the case of NATO membership—Partnership for Peace offered instead, and of cost, especially for agricultural support in the case of the EU, where only the most developed countries eg Hungary are likely to be admitted in the near future
- Accept any other valid points.

(*b*) Candidates are required to provide arguments and evidence to support a point of view. Candidates are also required to explain why the other option was rejected.

Accept from Source 1

For UK membership

EU takes over half UK exports which could be threatened following withdrawal.

Against

UK contributions are greater than receipts.

Accept from Source 2

For

CAP guarantees against food shortage

CAP reform is reducing cost/waste

CAP is helpful to poorest farmers including Scots crofters

More countryside improvement schemes

Against

CAP takes up half the budget and will continue to be biggest item

Surplus food often wasted or sold at a loss

Fewer UK workers are on farms compared to EU average

UK farms are more efficient than other regions of EU

4. (*b*) continued

Accept from Source 3

For

EU figures for working week, increase in earning and GDP are better than UK

EU has shorter working week than Japan and higher earnings than USA; both outwith EU

Against

UK unemployment and inflation are below EU average

the 2 economies outwith the EU both have lower inflation, higher GDP and lower unemployment, are better on improvements in earnings while Japan has better earnings growth.

Accept from Source 4

For

Much of the UK including nearly all of Scotland receives EU financial help. Some other areas such as Germany do less well

Against

Several countries such as Spain receive assistance without exceptions. Parts of the UK especially in England get no assistance

Credit highly integrated answers that link sources

Also accept any other valid points.

Modern Studies
Credit Level
1999

1. (*a*) The concept being assessed is **Participation**. Candidates are expected to use their understanding of the concept to provide explanations in depth and detail.

"Good points" include:

- They can join political parties
- They can go to public meetings held by political parties
- They can stand as candidates
- They can canvass on behalf of a political party
- The can leaflet on behalf of a political party
- Credit other valid points

(*b*) Candidates are required to explain instances of the **selective use of facts**, giving developed arguments based on evidence.

"Good points" include:

- It is the case that Helen Page has chosen to base her assertion on the results for fees for lobbying and being paid for asking parliamentary questions, where there is an overwhelming majority. However, that is not the case in the others

Modern Studies
Credit Level
1999 (cont.)

1. (b) continued

- The result for continuing with a trade or profession shows that there is a majority in favour of them carrying on with their interests. 45%–33%
- If you look at the results in the other categories, with the "No strong opinion" added in, there is no majority, never mind a clear majority

(c) The candidate is required to make comparisons within a complex source and draw valid conclusions.

"Good points" include:

- More men than women belong to trade unions
- Less than 1/3 of employees are members of trade unions
- The older you are the more likely you are to be in a trade union
- Employees from the black community are more likely to be in trade unions than any other ethnic group
- Employees from Pakistani/Bangla Deshi community are poorly represented in trade unions

2. (a)

The concept being assessed is **Equality**. Candidates are expected to explain how various factors interact to affect individuals and/or groups.

"Good points" include:

- Large number of jobs created by "hi-tec" industries in certain parts of Scotland
  - manufacture and assembly of components
  - servicing of equipment
- New types of jobs created as a result of "footloose" nature of new technology—eg call centres
- Opportunity for working from home for some business people
- Any other relevant point

Award maximum of 4 marks if candidate deals **only** with job creation **or** losses however contrasts may be implicit.

(b) The concept being assessed is **Ideology**. Candidates are expected to use their understanding of the concept to provide explanations in depth and detail.

"Good points" include:

Arguments for

- points relating to "social justice" arguments
- in line with European legislation and other major countries
- government policy at 1997 General Election—part of manifesto

2. (b) continued

Arguments against

- may lead to loss of competitiveness for British business
- may lead to unemployment as companies seek to become more efficient

Credit any other valid points.

(c) (i) Candidates are required to formulate a hypothesis

For example:

- Single Parents are more likely than other groups to be unemployed
- Single Parents are more likely than other groups to have a part-time job
- Child Minding costs mean that many single parents choose not to work

(ii) Candidates are required to state aims/headings relevant to an investigation

For example:

- Average wages for single parents
- Unemployment rates for single parents
- The cost of childminding

(iii) Candidates are required to provide a detailed description of an appropriate method of enquiry.

Internet

- Locate computer with access to the Internet (eg School Library, Public Library, Cyber Cafe, Home etc)
- Use of search engines
- Identification of websites of relevant organisations
- Download of print relevant material
- Use of e-mail to contact appropriate bodies/individuals
- any other relevant points

Interview

- Prepare detailed questions in advance
- Recording letters eg tape recorder, notebook etc
- Contacts with interviewee
- Location of interview
- Any other relevant points

(iv) Candidates are required to demonstrate an awareness of the benefits/limitations of a method of enquiry.

Expect reference to:

Internet

Reasons for

- access to massive range of information
- immediacy of access
- e-mail facility

Reasons against

- Inefficiency of many search mechanisms
- Lack of access to computers
- Cost of accessing telephone line
- Potentially biased information

Credit any other valid points

2. (c) (iv) continued

Interview

Reasons for

- In-depth questioning—detailed answers
- First hand experiences of single parent
- Opportunity to supplement/modify questions during interview

Reasons against

- Possible difficulty in finding interview subject
- One person may not be representative
- May become emotional/too involved

Credit any other valid points

A—THE USA

3. (a) The concept being assessed is **Rights and Responsibilities**. Candidates are expected to use their understanding of the concept to provide explanations in depth and detail.

"Good points" include:

- right to vote
- right to stand for office
- freedom of speech to criticise the government and put forward political views
- freedom of the press
- right to form political parties
- right to lobby government
- right freedom of assembly, to demonstrate legally and the right to non-violent protest

(b) The skill being assessed is the ability of candidates to **draw conclusions**.

"Good points" include:

- In both central city areas and in suburban areas, Whites are more likely to own their own homes, ie 56% for Whites compared to 33% for Hispanics in central cities and 74% of Whites own their own homes compared to only 51% of Hispanics in suburban areas
- The houses lived in by Whites are worth more than the houses lived in by Hispanics in both central city areas and in suburban areas
- Hispanics' houses are more overcrowded as 29% in central cities and 27% of houses in suburban areas have more than one person per room, while the figure for Whites is only 2%.

(c) The skill being assessed is the ability of candidates to detect and explain **selective use of facts**.

"Good points" include:

- Source 1 indicates that between 1996 and 1997 the rate of unemployment has fallen over the US as a whole from 4.6% to 4.5% and has fallen in five out of the six regions shown

A 3. (c) continued

- Source 2 indicates that the IMF believe that the US Government is not damaging the US economy because the American growth rate has increased from 1.6% in 1995 to 4.9% in 1997, there has been a decline in the rise in the cost of living, government borrowing has fallen to less than half of its 1992 level in 1997 and the value of the US dollar has increased by about 5% all indicating success in the American economy
- Source 3 shows that only 19% of Americans worried about losing their job in 1997 compared with 30% in 1996, 80% did not worry about losing their job. Only a minority of all groups thought that the US was going through a period of bad times while more than half of all Americans and 59% of men thought it was going through a period of good times

B—RUSSIA

3. (a) The candidate is required to explain instances of **selective use of facts**, giving developed arguments.

"Good points" include:

- Source 1 Evidence that the economy is not working would include increase in unemployment, increase in strikes, increase in prices
- Source 2 Government supporters only have 12% support compared to 20% for Communists, 17% for Nationalists and large number of Don't knows
- Source 3 Unemployment is up, 25% of people are below the poverty line, serious health problems, crime increase, corruption, shortage of decent housing etc.

(b) The concept being assessed is **Rights and Responsibilities**. Candidates are expected to use their understanding of the concept to provide explanations in depth and detail. Credit reference to:

- Right to vote in free elections
- Right to stand for office
- Right to form/belong to political parties
- Right to demonstrate
- Right to freedom of speech and of the media

(c) The skill being assessed is to make comparisons within a source and draw valid conclusions.

"Good points" include:

- Differences in economic growth—varies from 2.9% in St Petersburg to 6.3% in Moscow
- Households with phone—chances of having a phone are much higher in Moscow/St Petersburg than in Irkutsk
- Income per head—people in Moscow have an average income of $3,916 more than those in Nizhny Novgorod
- Moscow citizens are much richer than those in other cities

Modern Studies
Credit Level
1999 (cont.)

C—CHINA

3. (a) Candidates are required to detect and explain selective use of facts.

"Good points" include:

Source 1

- % of low income decreasing
- % of high income increasing
- so income improving and changes have worked

Source 2

- % illiterate or primary only decreasing
- % secondary increasing
- % university or college increasing
- so education improving and changes have worked

Source 3

- improved living standards and can be linked to improving education in source 2
- improved medical care
- infant mortality decreasing
- so reforms working
- National Poverty Plan introduced and can be linked to increasing incomes in source 1
- so reforms continuing
- some people worse off
- increased reform will cause unemployment
- crime and violence continue to increase
- so reforms not working

Therefore peasant being selective in the use of facts.

Credit highly candidates who link the sources.

(b) The concept being assessed is **Rights and Responsibilities**. Candidates are expected to use their understanding of the concept to provide explanations in depth and detail.

"Good points" include:

The right to:

- have political parties with different opinions on running the country is limited
- free elections is limited as they are controlled by the Communist Party
- political protest and demonstration is limited as they are often crushed by the government
- dissent is severely limited as political dissidents can be imprisoned
- freedom is limited as the Communist Party only allows 'freedom within limits', its own limits
- Freedom of speech is limited as the media is strictly controlled by the Communist Party

Credit candidates who point out that the limits on political rights are changing in China today.

C 3. (c) Candidates are required to make comparisons between sources and draw conclusions from them.

"Good points" include:

Hunan Province

- middle political prisoners
- middle illiterate rate
- middle life expectancy
- middle infants deaths
- middle increase in wealth

Tibet

- most political prisoners
- highest illiterate rate
- lowest life expectancy
- highest infant deaths
- highest increase in wealth

Hong Kong

- lowest political prisoners
- lowest illiterate rate
- highest life expectancy
- lowest infant deaths
- lowest increase in wealth

The candidate needs to mention that the regions are different when compared to each other. Tibet has mostly negatives but has the best increase in wealth, Hong Kong has mostly positives with Hunan Province being between these two regions.

4. (a) The concept being assessed is **Need**. Candidates are required to give detailed explanations.

"Good points" include:

- aid following disasters
- education projects providing African people with opportunity to train as specialists/experts etc
- agricultural projects (seeds, tools, methods), enabling Africans to produce their own crops
- industrial projects such as hydro-electricity plants enabling development of industrial bases
- training of medical staff to treat own people and provisions of health centres for long-term health
- any other valid points

Credit discussion of problems/difficulties of aid but do not insist on it.

(b) The candidate is required to provide arguments/evidence for and against a chosen view using complex sources. The candidate must also give an overall view of whether or not the evidence supports the view.

4. (b) continued

"Good points" include:

For the view

Source 1

- some countries are still military dictatorships
- corruption and threats are still being used in elections
- civil war still affects a number of African countries

Source 2

- wealth in Ethiopia and Nigeria has gone down
- external debt has increased over the decade shown
- in South Africa and Congo-Zaire there has been negative economic growth

Source 3

- in three countries calorie intake is below the recommended level
- calories per person has dropped in three countries
- infant mortality in South Africa has increased
- spending on education has decreased as % of wealth in Nigeria

Source 4

- Ethiopia imports more goods than it exports many countries in Africa shown on the map import more goods than they export

Against the view

Source 1

- twelve countries have become democracies
- many countries now hold multi-party elections or are limited democracies

Source 2

- wealth per person has increased in Zaire and South Africa
- economic growth has improved in Ethiopia and Nigeria

Source 3

- Ethiopia, Nigeria and Zaire have reduced infant mortality rates
- Ethiopia has increased spending on education

Source 4

- South Africa, Nigeria, Congo-Zaire and other countries in Africa shown on the map have a trade surplus

Modern Studies
Credit Level
2000

1.   (a)   The concept being assessed is **Representation**. Detailed explanations are required.

Answers may include:

FPTP

- Strong government as the winning party will, on most occasions, have an overall majority.

1. (a) continued

- Easy to understand by the electorate as they only have one choice to make.
- The candidate with most votes wins.
- Direct link between elected representatives and constituency

AMS

- It gives a fairer result as an element of proportionality is included.
- Voters are given more choice as they now have two votes and can vote for individuals in different parties if they wish.
- Coalition governments might mean that parties have to co-operate and work with one another, leading to consensus politics.
- Similar system is used in other countries such as Germany, where it has led to stable democracy.
- Any other valid point.

(b)   The concept being assessed is **Participation**. Detailed explanations are required.

Answers may include:

- The United Kingdom is a democracy and for democracy to flourish people must get involved and the most straightforward way is by voting in elections.
- If people do not vote then they really have no real right to criticise what an individual, party or government is doing.
- Many people fought long and hard in the past so that people today would have the fundamental right to vote which was denied to so many people in the past.
- Any other valid point.

(c)   The skill being assessed is the ability to formulate a hypothesis.

For example:

All Pressure Groups use the same methods to influence MPs

Some Pressure Group methods have been more effective than others

Some Pressure Group methods are illegal.

(d)   The skill being assessed is the ability to state aims or headings relevant to the issue.

For example:

Hypothesis—Some Pressure Group Methods are more effective than others.

Aims—What methods do Pressure Groups use? Which methods have proved to be the most effective?

Hypothesis—MPs are easily influenced by Pressure Group activities.

Aims—To show examples where MPs have changed their opinion because of Pressure Groups. To show which MPs are members of Pressure Groups.

Modern Studies
Credit Level
2000 (cont.)

1. (e) The skill being assessed is the ability to describe how the given method might be used.

Answers may include:

- Looking up reference books for information

- Borrowing books to take home for personal study

- Accessing the Internet to look at relevant web-sites

- Using e-mail facilities to contact MPs and Pressure Groups

- Using CD ROM material stored in libraries

- Any other valid point

(f) The skill being assessed is the ability to demonstrate an awareness of the benefits/limitations of a method of enquiry.

- Level of response to a questionnaire may be poor, therefore difficult to draw conclusions from responses

- Respondents may not give honest answers

- Some respondents may refuse to answer certain questions

- If questionnaire is done by post then it is relatively expensive for an individual to carry out

- Answers from Pressure Group may be biased

- Any other valid point

2. (a) The concept being assessed is **Need**. Detailed explanations are required.

Answers may include:

- Many elderly have serious health problems and nursing home gives them 24 hour care from trained nurses.

- Many elderly are too frail to cook meals, and meet their needs; in residential care, all their needs can be met by staff.

- Residential care provides company.

- Many elderly have no family to move in with.

- Sheltered housing accepts only those who can look after themselves.

- Any other valid reason.

(b) The skill being assessed is the ability to explain instances of selective use of facts, giving developed arguments.

2. (b) continued

Reference should be made to:

- Source 1
  - shows that between 1980s and 1990s there have been changes in sources of income with less than half now coming from state benefits and the amount from occupation pensions rising from 16% to 25%, with a small increase in investment income but less from paid work.

- Source 2
  - shows that women are likely to be poorer than men
  - that recently retired pensioners are likely to be better off than older pensioners
  - that the richest of pensioners increased their income by 81% but the poorest rose only by 28%

- Source 3
  - many pensioners in the UK do not meet their needs easily—only 44% say they are very well-off
  - in Denmark and Netherlands more pensioners are very well-off than in the UK

(c) The concept being assessed is **Equality**. Detailed explanations are required.

Answers may include:

- Lack of child care facilities/or facilities with suitable hours

- Cost of child care facilities too high for those with low-paid jobs and many women are in this type of job.

- Prejudice and discrimination by employers—eg worry about prospect of lone parents taking time off work if children ill/holiday problem.

- Need for part-time job to fit school hours/holidays

- Any other valid reason

A—THE USA

3. (a) The skill being assessed is the ability to make comparisons within and between complex sources and draw valid conclusions from them, with justification by developed argument when required.

Answers may include:

Source 1

- New York has much larger population than others (18·2 million, compared to 2·8 million and 0·6 million)

- New York has much larger proportion of urban population than the others (92%, compared to 44% and 28%)

- States with smaller population have greater proportion of rural inhabitants (eg Iowa, Vermont)

3 A. (*a*) continued

Source 2

- New York has a much higher violent crime rate than Iowa or Vermont

- New York has a higher proportion of prisoners in its population

Source 3

- New York has a higher average income ($27,000) than Iowa or Vermont

- Unemployment is higher in New York than in Iowa or Vermont

- New York has a higher proportion of the population living below the poverty line than Iowa or Vermont

Source 4

- New York has more people without health insurance

- New York has more doctors per head of population

- Infant death rate higher in New York

- More births to mothers under 20 in Iowa and Vermont

- Any other valid points

Very high marks would be given for comparing and linking the sources in the following ways:

- State with high urban population also has higher crime rate and proportion of prisoners (Sources 1 and 2)

- State with higher urban population also has less employment (Sources 1 and 3)

- States with larger rural population have less crime (Sources 1 and 2)

- States with larger rural population have more employment (Sources 1 and 3)

- States with larger rural population have lower average incomes (Sources 1 and 3)

- Higher urban population and/or poverty linked to percentage of population with no health insurance (Sources 1, 2 and 3)

- Higher rural population linked to a larger number of births to mothers aged under 20

- Any other valid points

(*b*) The skill being assessed is the ability to detect and explain examples of lack of objectivity in complex sources, giving developed argument when required.

Answers may include:

- Source 1 shows that Blacks are 13·0% of the population but are only 8·6% of the House of Representatives, 0·0% of the Senate and 6·9% of total in Congress and so Blacks are not fairly represented.

3 A. (*b*) continued

    or similar comments about Hispanics, Asian/Pacific Islanders or Native Americans who are also under represented.

- Source 2 shows that men are the vast majority in the House of Representatives. 379 men to 56 women and so women are not fairly represented **or** similar comment about the senate.

(*c*) The concept being assessed is **Ideology**. Detailed explanations are required.

Answers may include:

- Freedom of speech and freedom of assembly

- Freedom of the press

- Freedom to participate in the political system

- Freedom of movement

- Protection against discrimination

- The right to a fair trial

- The right to carry a gun for self-protection

- Any other valid point.

B—RUSSIA

3 B.   (*a*) The skill being assessed is the ability to detect and explain examples of lack of objectivity in complex sources, giving developed argument when required.

Answers may include:

- Source 1 shows that in the 1993 Duma elections no party had a clear lead and that coalition government was required

- Source 1 shows that in the 1995 Duma elections there was no clear winner and that coalition government was required

- Sources 1 and 2 show that "other" parties did well in both elections, suggesting no clear view about which party should control the Duma

- Source 2 shows that the leading candidate in the 1996 Presidential Election got only 35·3% of the votes

- Source 2 shows that the two leading candidates were very close

- Any other valid point.

(*b*) The skill being assessed is the ability to make comparisons within and between complex sources and draw valid conclusions from them, with justification by developed argument when required.

Answers may include:

Source 1

- Economic inequality between Moscow and Krasnoyarsk—particularly in terms of foreign investment

- Suggestion that politicians are biased towards the Moscow area and that poorer areas subsidise the capital

Modern Studies
Credit Level
2000 (cont.)

3 B. (b) continued

Source 2

- Wage arrears and underpayment in Moscow are less serious than in other parts of Russia

Source 3

- In Moscow there are less new permanent jobs available—more are for fixed-term and casual than in the Chuvash Republic or in Chelyabinsk.

Source 4

- Yeltsin was much more popular in Moscow than in the other areas of Russia
- Zyuganov was very popular in the Chuvash Republic
- Zhirinovsky and Yavlinsky less popular throughout all areas
- Any other valid points.

Very high marks would be given for comparing and linking sources in the following ways:

- Yeltsin not popular in areas where there are wage arrears and underpayments (Sources 2 and 4)
- Yeltsin popular where wages are paid in full and on time (Sources 2 and 4)
- Communist leader popular in areas with economic problems (Sources 4 and 1, 2, 3)
- No strong political opinion in Krasnoyarsk, where people may be disillusioned with whole idea of Moscow government (Sources 1 and 4)
- Any other valid points.

(c) The concept being assessed is Ideology. Detailed explanations are required.

Answers may include:

- Freedom to travel outwith the country
- Freedom to join any political party of their choice
- Freedom of the press and media
- Freedom to demonstrate
- Freedom to vote for a variety of political parties
- Any other valid point.

C—CHINA

3 C. (a) The concept being assessed is **Ideology**. Detailed explanations are required.

Answers may include:

- Greater economic freedom, allowing some Chinese to greatly improve their standards of living

3 C. (a) continued

- More contact with the outside world, with access to foreign businesses and markets
- Clamp down on some groups such as the Falun Gong sect
- Limited democratisation in local politics
- Any other valid point.

(b) The skill being assessed is the ability to detect and explain examples of lack of objectivity in complex sources, giving developed argument when required.

Answers may include:

- Ordinary workers and farmers make up a total of 20·5% of the total, not the majority of deputies in the National People's Congress (Source 1)
- The Communist Party are the only strong party in the system—the others only have a tiny fraction of the membership of the Communist Party (Source 2)
- 79% of the deputies to the National People's Congress are male—this could be construed as a criticism of the Chinese political system (Source 1)
- Any other valid point.

(c) The skill being assessed is the ability to make comparisons within and between complex sources and draw valid conclusions from them, with justification by developed argument when required.

Answers may include:

Source 1

- Guangdong, Shanghai and Beijing all have a greater proportion of China's wealth than their proportion of the population

  Sichuan has less wealth than it should have, given the number of people who live there

Source 2

- Mobile phone ownership is highest in Guangdong
- Sichuan has a large population but low number of mobile phones
- Similar rate of mobile phone ownership in Beijing and Shanghai

Source 3

- Good access to tap water throughout China, but best in Beijing and Shanghai
- Much lower level of gas supply in Sichuan than the others. Sichuan well below national average
- Beijing has a very high provision of public toilets; Shanghai has a very poor provision

3 C. (c) continued

Source 4

- Rapid improvement in living standards in Guangdong and Shanghai
- Slow economic progress in rural areas such as Sichuan
- Any other valid points.

Very high marks would be given for comparing and linking sources in the following ways:

- Percentage of population with access to tap water linked to lower population (Sources 2 and 3)
- Areas where the proportion of wealth exceeds the proportion of population also have higher than national average supplies of gas, mobile phone ownership etc (Sources 1, 2 and 3)
- Any other valid points.

4. (a) The concept being assessed is **Power**. Detailed explanations are required.

Answers may include:

Arguments For

- Access to a wider market for companies and products from existing members
- Wider opportunity for work, study and travel by European citizens
- Greater contribution to pan-European economic cooperation and security

Arguments Against

- Britain and other richer members less likely to receive assistance from regional/social funds
- New members likely to receive most assistance from Common Agricultural Policy
- Large numbers of people may choose to come to live in wealthier countries
- Current EU structure needs reform rather than enlargement
- Any other valid points.

(b) (i) The skill being assessed is the ability to provide arguments and evidence for and against a point of view.

Answers may include:

ARGUMENTS FOR

- There are many security flashpoints in Europe—eg Montenegro, Cyprus, Kosovo (Source 1)
- Peace dividend has led to economic problems in Germany (Source 2)
- Unless military spending increases there will be wider economic problems (Source 2)
- Some nationalist problems have led to serious problems—eg Turkey, Yugoslavia (Source 3)

4. (b) (i) continued

ARGUMENTS
AGAINST

- Some flashpoints have been solved in a peaceful way—eg Germany, Baltic Republics (Source 1)
- Some nationalist problems have been solved peacefully—eg Czech/ Slovak split (Source 3)
- Military force did not bring about peace in Yugoslavia (Source 3)
- NATO actions can lead to many casualties and an escalation of violence (Source 4)
- Any other valid points— provided they are based on the source material

Very high marks would be awarded to integrated answers that link sources.

(ii) The skill being assessed is the ability to provide an overall conclusion.

Two marks would be given if an overall conclusion is provided, and the explanation goes beyond repetition of the answer to (b).

One mark would be given if an overall conclusion is provided, but the explanation is largely repetition of parts of the answer to (b) or is very generalised.

Explanations should be based on the Source material but may develop it beyond what is stated explicitly in the sources.

Modern Studies
Credit Level
2001

1. (a) The concept being assessed is **Rights & Responsibilities**. Detailed descriptions are required.

Answers may include:

- The right to talk to management about the proposed job losses.
- The right to put forward to management alternative proposals which might limit the job losses.
- The right to take industrial action should the members wish that they do so. This can only happen after the correct legal procedures, including a secret ballot of the membership, have taken place.
- The major responsibility that they have is to act positively on behalf of their members.
- They also have a responsibility to remain within the law because the Trade Union could be sued by the company(s) or face legal action if they break the law by carrying out unofficial industrial action.
- Any other valid point.

Modern Studies
Credit Level
2001 (cont.)

1. *(b)* The skill being assessed is the ability to detect and explain examples of lack of objectivity in complex sources, giving developed argument when required.

Answers may include:

- Women's issues are way down the pecking order at 4%—only a slight increase on ten years ago.

- Pay is an issue of real concern but its importance has declined over the ten year period by 6% to 22%.

- Working conditions only rank third in order of importance. This is well behind the protection of existing jobs. The percentage has stayed constant at 21%.

- Any other valid point.

(c) The skill being assessed is the ability to make comparisons within and between complex sources and draw valid conclusions from them, with justification by developed argument when required.

For 8 marks both sources must be used, otherwise a maximum of 6 marks would be given.

Answers that repeat the source material without making comparisons and/or drawing conclusions would be awarded zero marks.

Answers may include:

- In some parts of Scotland the Labour Party swept the board in the constituencies eg in Glasgow and the West of Scotland they won all the seats.

- The Highlands and Islands is a Liberal Democrat stronghold where they won five of the constituency seats.

- The Conservative Party did not win any of the constituency seats anywhere in Scotland.

- An independent candidate was able to beat the major parties in one constituency.

- Labour got less than 40% of the popular vote in the constituencies yet picked up 53 out of the 73 seats available.

- The SNP were only 10% behind in the popular vote but were only able to secure seven constituency seats.

- The Liberal Democrats targeted particular constituencies which meant 14% of the popular vote got them 12 constituency seats

1. *(c)* continued

- The Regional List which was elected by proportional representation was instrumental in gaining 28 seats for the SNP which meant that they became the official opposition.

- The Conservatives' reasonable showing in terms of the popular vote meant that they got 18 seats from the Regional List.

- Small parties such as the Greens and the Scottish Socialists got representation in Edinburgh through the list system.

- Labour support is particularly strong in the central belt.

- Any other valid point.

2. *(a)* The concept being assessed is **Equality**. Detailed explanations are required.

Answers may include:

- Differences in employment—some jobs have higher incomes than others.

- Number of adults working—lone parent families have only one income.

- Child care costs—lone parents may have to pay for expensive child care with an effect on their standard of living.

- Number of children in the family.

- Cost of living in the area that they come from.

- Educational attainment of parents—influences their later earning potential.

- Any other valid point.

(b) The concept being assessed is **Ideology**. Detailed explanations are required.

Answers may include:

- New Deal Programmes.

- Young unemployed get subsidised employment, full time education and/or training, voluntary work, environmental work.

- Long-term unemployed—personal advisors, options of subsidised employment and education/training.

- Lone parents—extra benefits, subsidised nursery places, after school and holiday clubs.

- Over 50s—employment credits etc.

- Tax and benefit changes to make work more attractive.

- National Minimum Wage to attract people into work.

- Area-based schemes such as Employment Action Zones

- Any other valid point.

(c) The skill being assessed is the ability to detect and explain examples of lack of objectivity in complex sources, giving developed argument when required.

2. (c) continued

For 8 marks all three sources must be used.

Answers may include:

Source 1

- Does not benefit employers as they are forced to put wages up thereby increasing their costs.
- Lost benefits of running own business through government interference.

Source 2

- Does not benefit all employees as NMW does not apply to some people—particularly the young workers.
- Some employers do not pay the agreed rates.
- Reduction in the number of jobs and in the number of working hours.
- UK still below European poverty levels.

Source 3

- Although fewer female workers earn less than £3·60 per hour in 1999 many do still earn less than that, especially in the hotel and catering industry.
- Bar staff appear to have benefited most from the introduction of the NMW.
- Any other valid point.

A—THE USA

3 A. (a)   The concept being assessed is **Participation**. Detailed descriptions are required.

Answers may include:

- Voting for representatives—County, State and Federal Levels.
- Standing to be a representative at any of these levels.
- Taking part in the election process by campaigning, fund-raising etc.
- Being an election worker—helping with the count.
- Any other valid point.

(b)   The concept being assessed is **Equality**. Detailed descriptions are required.

Answers may include:

- Less prejudice and discrimination in wide variety of areas, eg education, housing, employment.
- Ethnic minority groups given legal equality.
- Better education has led to improved job prospects and earnings potential.
- Affirmative Action programmes.
- Successful economy means that ethnic minorities are not marginalized as they might be during a recession.
- Increasing representation for ethnic minority groups at all levels of government.
- Any other valid point.

3 A. (c)   The skill being assessed is the ability to formulate a hypothesis.

The following are worth 1 mark:

- Men and women have equal opportunities in the USA.
- Men and women do not have equal opportunities in the USA.

The following are worth 2 marks:

- Men and women have equal opportunities in politics in the USA.
- Men and women do not have equal opportunities in employment in the USA.
- The income gap between men and women in the USA is closing.

(d)   The skill being assessed is the ability to state aims or headings relevant to the issue.

Hypothesis:

Men and women have equal opportunities in politics in the USA.

Aims:

What are the numbers of men and women in Congress?

Do Senators in the USA think that men and women have equal chances of being elected?

Hypothesis:

Men and women have equal opportunities in employment.

Aims:

To find out the percentage of men and women in different kinds of work in the USA.

To find out what men and women are paid in similar jobs in the USA.

(e)   The skill being assessed is the ability to describe how the given method might be used.

No marks would be awarded if the way described is inappropriate to an investigation on the topic of equal opportunities.

Answers may include:

- Log on to World Wide Web after gaining permission from teacher.
- Find appropriate web site through use of search engine or bookmarks.
- Use sites such as Library of Congress or White House for political information and statistics.
- Send e-mail questions to organisations/individuals. E-mail addresses of Senators and Representatives may be available on the web.
- Any other valid point.

Modern Studies
Credit Level
2001 (cont.)

3 A. *(f)* The skill being assessed is the ability to demonstrate an awareness of the benefits of a method of enquiry.

Answers may include:

- Easy to access American sources which would otherwise be hard to get.
- Much quicker than sending letters to American sources.
- Internet available in most schools and in many homes.
- E-mail allows virtually instant contact with American sources.
- Information can be printed off to look at later.
- Easy to access American magazines and newspapers—eg Time, Newsweek, New York Herald, Washington Post etc.
- Any other valid point.

(g) The skill being assessed is the ability to demonstrate an awareness of the limitations of a method of enquiry.

Answers may include:

- There might be too much information and it would take a long time to find the good articles.
- They could all be mixed up and in no particular order. They might not be organised by date or topic.
- Some candidates would contend that their Modern Studies teacher is very untidy and it is highly unlikely that the material will be sorted, have dates etc.
- Information might be out of date.
- Any other valid point.

B—RUSSIA

3 B. *(a)* The concept being assessed is **Participation**. Detailed descriptions are required.

Answers may include:

- Voting for representatives—at local and national level.
- Standing to be a representative at any of these levels.
- Taking part in the election process by campaigning, fund-raising for any of the major parties etc.
- Being an election worker—helping with the count.
- Any other valid point.

(b) The concept being assessed is **Equality**. Detailed descriptions are required.

Answers may include:

- Food prices have increased dramatically.
- Some sectors of the workforce are not paid regularly.

3 B. *(b)* continued

- Variations in unemployment and wage levels across the country.
- Employees of foreign firms well paid.
- Any other valid point.

(c) The skill being assessed is the ability to formulate a hypothesis.

The following are worth 1 mark:

- Men and women are equal in Russia.
- Russians are all treated equally.

The following are worth 2 marks:

- Men and women in Russia are treated equally in employment.
- Women receive equal pay for equal work in Russia.

(d) The skill being assessed is the ability to state aims or headings relevant to the issue.

Hypothesis:

Men and women in Russia are treated equally by employers.

Aims:

To find out about equality laws in Russia.

Male and female holiday entitlement in Russia.

Hypothesis:

Women receive equal pay for equal work in Russia.

Aims:

Wage levels for male and female employees in Russia.

What types of jobs do women do in Russia?

(e) The skill being assessed is the ability to describe how the given method might be used.

Answers may include:

- Log on to World Wide Web after gaining permission from teacher.
- Find appropriate web site through use of search engine or bookmarks.
- Use sites such as Russian Embassy for political information and statistics.
- Send e-mail questions to organisations/individuals. E-mail addresses of Russian figures may be available on the web.
- Any other valid point.

(f) The skill being assessed is the ability to demonstrate an awareness of the benefits of a method of enquiry.

Answers may include:

- Easy to access Russian sources which would otherwise be hard to get.
- Much quicker than sending letters to Russian sources.
- Internet available in most schools and in many homes.

3 B. (f) continued

- E-mail allows virtually instant contact with Russian sources.
- Information can be printed off to look at later.
- Easy to access Russian magazines and newspapers.
- Any other valid point.

(g) The skill being assessed is the ability to demonstrate an awareness of the limitations of a method of enquiry.

Answers may include:

- There might be too much information and it would take a long time to find the good articles.
- They could all be mixed up and in no particular order. They might not be organised by date or topic.
- Some candidates would contend that their Modern Studies teacher is very untidy and it is highly unlikely that the material will be sorted, have dates etc.
- Information might be out of date.
- Any other valid point.

C—CHINA

3 C. (a) The concept being assessed is **Participation**. Detailed descriptions are required.

Answers may include:

- Voting in elections for village committees which take place every three years.
- Voting on issues discussed within Neighbourhood Committees.
- Voting for candidates for the Local People's Congress who then send delegates to the National People's Congress.
- Showing support for candidates and parties (usually the Communist Party).
- Any other valid point.

(b) The concept being assessed is **Equality**. Detailed descriptions are required.

Answers may include:

- In the countryside the responsibility system has allowed enterprising farmers to become richer, but increased mechanisation has led to rural unemployment.
- In some rural areas there is a shortage of labour due to migration to the cities.
- Many Chinese businesses are now privately owned allowing the owner to make a profit.
- Some people migrating to the cities find wealth and success; others find poverty and destitution.
- Any other valid point.

3 C. (c) The skill being assessed is the ability to formulate a hypothesis.

The following are worth 1 mark:

- Men and women have equal opportunities in China.
- Chinese people are all treated equally.

The following are worth 2 marks:

- Men and women in China do equally well in education.
- Women have achieved political equality in China.

(d) The skill being assessed is the ability to state aims or headings relevant to the issue.

Hypothesis:

In China women do as well as men in education.

Aims:

To find out how well girls do at school compared to boys.

How many women go on to university in China?

Hypothesis:

Women have achieved political equality in China.

Aims:

Do women vote as much as men in China?

How many women are members of the Chinese government?

(e) The skill being assessed is the ability to describe how the given method might be used.

Answers may include:

- Log on to World Wide Web after gaining permission from teacher.
- Find appropriate web site through use of search engine or bookmarks.
- Use sites such as Chinese Embassy for political information and statistics.
- Send e-mail questions to organisations/individuals. E-mail addresses of Chinese figures may be available on the web.
- Any other valid point.

(f) The skill being assessed is the ability to demonstrate an awareness of the benefits of a method of enquiry.

Answers may include:

- Easy to access Chinese sources which would otherwise be hard to get.
- Much quicker than sending letters to Chinese sources.
- Internet available in most schools and in many homes.
- E-mail allows virtually instant contact with Chinese sources.
- Information can be printed off to look at later.
- Easy to access Chinese magazines and newspapers.
- Any other valid point.

Modern Studies
Credit Level
2001 (cont.)

3 C.   (*g*)   The skill being assessed is the ability to demonstrate an awareness of the limitations of a method of enquiry.

Answers may include:

- There might be too much information and it would take a long time to find the good articles.

- They could all be mixed up and in no particular order. They might not be organised by date or topic.

- Some candidates would contend that their Modern Studies teacher is very untidy and it is highly unlikely that the material will be sorted, have dates etc.

- Information might be out of date.

- Any other valid point.

4.   (*a*)   The concept being assessed is **Power**. Detailed explanations are required.

Answers may include:

- Debt repayment—poorer African countries may be made to make debt repayments on loans from richer countries.

- Trade agreements—poorer countries have to sell commodities (including food products and mineral products) to richer countries at the price offered by the richer countries. The strong bargaining position lies with the richer nations.

- Aid—some aid given by richer countries is in the form of "tied" or "boomerang" aid. Conditions are attached which mean that the money is recycled to the economy of the richer country and the way it is spent may not be of most benefit to the poorer countries.

- Aid packages offered by richer countries, either in the form of bilateral or through multi-lateral aid, may not be a massive part of the overall spending for these countries, but they do have a major impact on the income of poorer nations. Decisions to reduce or increase aid spending having a much wider impact than is imagined in the richer countries.

- Political influence—due to the colonial legacy, some European countries still regard parts of Africa as being within their "sphere of influence".

- Military influence—where European countries have a military involvement in disputes, then leaders of African countries may "owe" favours in return for the support.

- Any other valid point.

4.   (*b*)   The skill being assessed is the ability to provide arguments and evidence to support a personal point of view.

For full marks, all three sources must be used.

Answers may include:

For Option One: Helicopters and pilots to be sent to Mozambique.

- "The most urgent problem is to rescue thousands of people who have become stranded on isolated areas of higher ground . . ." figures suggest that more helicopters are required. (Source 1)

- Mozambique's army only has small assault helicopters—there are no large personnel-carrying helicopters. (Source 2)

- IRC says that the number of helicopters is not enough. (Source 2)

- "Planes flying over Mozambique could not land where help was most needed." (Source 3)

- Helicopters can also help in the rebuilding of the infrastructure (implied in various sources)

For Option Two: Send teams of engineers to Mozambique.

- "Many important road bridges have been swept away and some areas have been cut-off completely. Mozambique has appealed for aid to help rebuild the transport and communication system." (Source 1)

- Rebuilding the infrastructure will help the distribution of food. (Source 2)

- Guardian newspaper highlighted the question "Why are troops not mending the roads?" Main road, vital for distributing food, medicines etc, blocked in five places. (Source 3)

- Repair of roads and bridges is the most immediate need, according to graph. (Source 3)

- Any other valid point.

(*c*)   The skill being assessed is the ability to provide arguments and evidence to support a personal point of view.

For 2 marks a NEW point should be included that was not included in the answer to (*b*), or make a very good generalised point based on the Sources.

1 mark would be given where the candidate repeats information from their answer to (*b*) with little or no development.

Zero marks would be given where the candidate makes no attempt to justify their point from the sources.

For example:

I rejected Option 2 because Option 1 is better at meeting the needs of Mozambique.

I rejected Option 1 because it is no use.

Modern Studies
Credit Level
2002

1. (*a*)   The concept being assessed is **Representation**. Candidates are required to use understanding of the concept to provide detailed explanations with relevant examples and appropriate generalisations.

"Good points" include:

- Asking a Parliamentary question
- Initiating a debate
- Moving an amendment to a Bill
- Introducing a Member's Bill
- Contacting a Minister
- Meeting a Minister
- Any other valid point

(*b*)   (i) and (ii)

Candidates are required to express support for a personal point of view with a developed argument.

In (i) candidates must refer to **at least one** of the sources and the information about Marchglen Constituency.

"Good points" include:

Jean Alder

- Experience as a trade union negotiator dealing with factory closures would be useful in dealing with the threatened closure of the large textile factory and with helping to raise wages in the new industries
- Visited Japan several times, so could be useful in helping to attract the Japanese company which would be good for dealing with unemployment in the constituency
- Campaign speech promises to work for more money for retraining which is needed as traditional industries have closed and the skills needed now are for jobs in the call centre and computer assembly plant
- Speech promises to campaign for public transport so local people campaigning for re-opening of the railway would be pleased
- Any other valid point

Jennifer Wood

- Experience as a local councillor, background and role in last election, could make her a better candidate for defeating the SNP
- Involvement as a councillor in attracting the American computer company is useful experience to use in attracting the Japanese company
- She speaks three languages so this could be good with the project to attract more foreign businesses to the area
- She campaigns on the environment, so would deal with the concerns on pollution from the chemical waste disposal company

1. (*b*) continued

- She promises to attract small businesses which could help deal with the problem of unemployment
- She promises to campaign to raise the National Minimum Wage to £5 per hour which would be attractive to those who are paid below the Scottish average in Marchglen
- Any other valid point

(ii)   It is **not** necessary to make an explicit link between the sources and the information about Marchglen to gain 2 marks.

Do not credit points that have already been made in the answer to (*b*)(i)

(*c*)   Candidates are requried to detect and explain examples of lack of objectivity, giving developed arguments where required.

"Good points" include:

- A big difference in the gender representation in the Labour Party with an even number of men and women in the Scottish Parliament but 45 men to only 11 women in the UK parliament
- A much greater representation of women in the SNP respresentation in Scotland compared to the UK Parliament
- A much greater representation of women in the Scottish Parliament with appropriate examples
- Any other valid point

2. (*a*)   The concepts being assessed are **equality and need**. Candidates are required to use understanding of the concepts to provide detailed explanations with relevant examples and appropriate generalisations.

"Good points" include:

- Health problems increase with age. Elderly people who are 75+ years old are more likely to suffer from illness than those aged 60–65
- The problems of those suffering from specific age-related illnesses such as arthritis, Alzheimer's are much greater than those of those elderly who do not suffer from them
- Link between poverty and ill-health means that poorer pensioners face greater health problems (eg nutrition-related illness, hypothermia)
- Wealthy older people may benefit from private health care
- Any other valid point

(*b*)   The concept being assessed is **Ideology**. Candidates are required to use understanding of the concept to provide detailed explanations with relevant examples and appropriate generalisations.

Modern Studies
Credit Level
2002 (cont.)

2. (b) continued

"Good points" include:

- At its present level the pension is too low to provide elderly people with a comfortable life style

- Pensioners who rely on the state pension alone cannot afford the standard of living expected in a modern society

- Many pensioners live in poverty and do not claim the additional benefits available to them. This means that they have an unnecessarily low standard of living. A higher basic pension would help to prevent this situation

- It is the job of government to provide pensioners with an adequate level of income—this argument would be used to counter claims that individuals should make greater use of private pension provision

- Any other valid point

(c)   Candidates are required to make comparisons within and between complex sources and draw valid conclusions from them, with justification by developed argument when required.

Credit highly interaction between sources. Both sources must be used.

Candidates who use information pertinent to other bullet-points in their answer to, for example, the second bullet point, should not be penalised for repetition.

"Good points" include:

Accommodation rates in different parts of Scotland (Source 2)

There is considerable variation in accommodation for elderly people in different parts of Scotland. Western Isles has the best provision for residential care home places but Glasgow City has the best provision of Special Needs Housing.

Ways in which accommodation for elderly people has changed since 1990 (Source 1)

There has been an increase in the provision of Special Needs Housing and Private Nursing Home places. Adapted housing has almost doubled in number. At the same time there has been a decrease in the number of places in Residential Care Homes and in the number of NHS Hospital Beds.
Overall there are many more places available for elderly people in 1999 than there were in 1990.

2. (c) continued

Number and use of NHS hospital beds (Source 1)

The number of NHS Hospital beds for elderly people has shown an overall decline from 1990 to 1999. Within the overall decline there has been an increase in the number of assessement beds (2521 to 3634) but a large decline in the number of residential beds (9277 to 4924).

Relationship between NHS hospital beds and other types of accommodation (Source 1)

In 1990 there were more residential NHS hospital beds for the elderly people in Scotland (9277) than there were local authority residential care home places (8807). By 1999 the situation was reversed. There were only 4924 residential NHS hospital beds for elderly people in Scotland but 6059 local authority residential care home places.

A—THE USA

3.   (a)   The concept being assessed is **Rights and Responsibilities**. Candidates are required to use understanding of the concept to provide detailed descriptions with relevant examples and appropriate generalisations.

"Good points" include:

- Right—to vote; Responsibility—to accept the elected President, Senator etc

- Right—to stand for election as a candidate; Responsibility—to campaign in a responsible way eg not be racist, prejudiced

- Right—to join an interest group, lobby, campaign, protest to influence the government. Responsibility—not to use violence or intimidation, eg anti-abortion hate campaigns against the family planning groups in the USA and against doctors who perform abortions

- Right—freedom of speech/press, eg People for the American Way who have an online newspaper focused on combating censorship in America's public schools; Responsibility—not to be racist or prejudiced and to tell the truth

- Right—freedom of assembly to protest; Responsibility—not to use violence, eg riot. To protest peacefully eg The Million Mom March in Washington and cities in the USA against gun ownership

(b)   Candidates are required to formulate a hypothesis

The following are worth 2 marks:

- Blacks and Hispanics are more likely than Whites to live in poorer housing and so do not get equality

- Hispanics do better in education than Blacks or Whites

A 3. (*b*) continued

• Blacks and Hispanics are less likely to be in poverty than Whites

Although this last example is probably factually inaccurate, it is a valid hypothesis

ie candidate has added something significant to the prompt

(*c*) Candidates are required to state aims or headings relevant to the issue.

For example:

Hypothesis: Blacks and Hispanics are more likely than Whites to live in poorer housing and so do not get equality

Aims: To find out what are the different kinds of housing found in an American city. To find out what is the percentage of Blacks, Hispanics and Whites living in these different kinds of housing

Hypothesis: Blacks and Hispanics are less likely to be in poverty than Whites.

Aims: To find out what are the different factors that produce poverty

To find out what is the percentage of Blacks, Hispanics and Whites living in poverty

(*d*) Candidates are required to demonstrate a method of enquiry for an investigation.

"Good points" include:

• I would use a search engine like Google to find good web sites on Equality in the USA. I would put in search terms like "Black, Hispanic and White poverty in the USA". The search engine might take my search to Quick Facts from the USA Census Bureau. I could click on the pages I found and use the best ones and print off their material

• On my computer at home I would go and look at the US Library of Congress/White House/USA Bureau of Statistics/USA Today web pages that I have book marked in my browser. I would use search options within these sites to find statistics on equality in the USA

• Any other valid point

(*e*) Candidates are required to demonstrate an awareness of the benefits of a method of enquiry.

• E-mail allows virtually instant contact with American sources and it is quite easy to find e-mail addresses. I could e-mail the Library of Congress for help in answering my questions

• I can e-mail questions directly to Ethnic Minority Americans in American schools if I log onto their school websites from the American Schools Directory

• Any other valid point

A 3. (*f*) Candidates are required to demonstrate an awareness of the limitations of a method of enquiry.

"Good points" include:

• There might be too much information for me to work through in school and my computer at home does not have a CD-ROM drive

• I might not have enough time to study all the information on the CD-ROMs as they might need to be shared between all of my class

• Information on the CD-ROMs may be out of date

• Any other valid point.

B—RUSSIA

3. (*a*) The concept being assessed is **Rights and Responsibilities**. Candidates are required to use understanding of the concept to provide detailed descriptions with relevant examples and appropriate generalisations.

"Good points" include:

• Right—to vote; Responsibility—to accept the elected President, Deputy etc

• Right—to stand for election as a candidate; Responsibility—to campaign in a responsible way eg not be racist, prejudiced

• Right—to join an interest group, lobby, campaign, protest to influence the government. Responsibility—not to use violence or intimidation, eg Chechen sympathisers carrying out terrorist attacks in Moscow

• Right—freedom of speech/press, eg new media freedoms in Russia allowing access to the internet etc; Responsibility—not to be racist or prejudiced and to tell the truth

• Right—freedom of assembly to protest; Responsibility—not to use violence, eg riot. To protest peacefully eg demonstrations against price rises and poverty

• Any other valid point

(*b*) Candidates are required to formulate a hypothesis.

The following are worth 2 marks:

• Older people with out of date skills are more likely than younger educated people to live in poorer housing and so do not get equality

• Russians do better in education than non-Russian groups

• Russians are less likely to be in poverty than non-Russian groups

Modern Studies
Credit Level
2002 (cont.)

B 3. (c) Candidates are required to state aims or headings relevant to the issue.

Hypothesis: Russians are more likely than non-Russians to live in poorer housing and so do not get equality

Aims: To find out what are the different kinds of housing found in a Russian city

To find out what is the percentage of Russians and non-Russians living in these different kinds of housing

Hypothesis: Russians are less likely to be in poverty than non-Russians

Aims: To find out what are the different factors that produce poverty

To find out what is the percentage of Russians and non-Russians living in poverty

(d) Candidates are required to describe how the given method might be used.

"Good points" include:

- I would use a search engine like Google to try to find good web sites on Equality in Russia. I would put in search terms like "Russia, Poverty, Wages, Equality". If I found good information I could save it to disk or print it off

- On my computer at home I would go and look at the Russian web pages that I have book marked in my browser. I would use search options within these sites to find statistics on equality in Russia

- Any other valid point

(e) Candidates are required to demonstrate an awareness of the benefits of a method of enquiry.

- E-mail allows virtually instant contact with Russian sources and it can be quite easy to find e-mail addresses. I could e-mail universities in Britain and America that specialise in Russian studies

- I can e-mail questions directly to schools and individuals in Russia through web-sites that list schools around the world

- Any other valid point

(f) Candidates are required to demonstrate an awareness of the limitations of a method of enquiry.

"Good points" include:

- There might be too much information for me to work through in school and my computer at home does not have a CD-ROM drive.

- I might not have enough time to study all the information on the CD-ROMS as they might need to be shared between all of my class.

- Information on the CD-ROMS may be out of date.

- Any other valid point

C—CHINA

3. (a) The concept being assessed is **Rights and Responsibilities**. Candidates are required to use understanding of the concept to provide detailed descriptions with relevant examples and appropriate generalisations.

"Good points" include:

- Political system is fundamentally undemocratic with too much power in the hands of the Communist Party

- Electoral changes at local level have not been reflected in national politics

- Dissent is not tolerated and dissidents are persecuted

- The legal and judicial system is flawed

- Chinese people lack the basic political rights enjoyed by most people around the world

- Any other valid point

(b) Candidates are required to formulate a hypothesis.

The following are worth 2 marks:

- Older people with out of date skills are more likely than younger educated people to live in poorer housing and so do not get equality

- Some parts of China do better in education than other parts

- Some parts of China are less likely to be in poverty than other parts

(c) Candidates are required to state aims or headings relevant to the issue.

Hypothesis: Some parts of China have poorer housing than others

Aims: To find out what are the different kinds of housing found in China

To find out what is the percentage of Chinese people living in different types and standards of housing

Hypothesis: Some parts of China have more poverty than other parts of the country

Aims: To find out what are the different factors that produce poverty

To find out what is the percentage of people living in poverty in different parts of China

(d) Candidates are required to describe how the given method might be used.

"Good points" include:

- I would use a search engine like Google to try to find good web sites on Equality in China. I would put in search terms like "China, Poverty, Wages, Equality". If I found good information I could save it to disk or print it off

- On my computer at home I would go and look at the Chinese web pages that I have book marked in my browser. I would use search options within these sites to find statistics on equality in China.

- Any other valid point

C 3. (e) Candidates are required to demonstrate an awareness of the benefits of a method of enquiry.

"Good points" include:

- E-mail allows virtually instant contact with Chinese sources and it can be quite easy to find e-mail addresses. I could e-mail universities in Britain and America that specialise in Chinese studies
- I can e-mail questions directly to schools and individuals in China through web-sites that list schools around the world
- Any other valid point

(f) Candidates are required to demonstrate an awareness of the limitations of a method of enquiry.

"Good points" include:

- There might be too much information for me to work through in school and my computer at home does not have a CD-ROM drive
- I might not have enough time to study all the information on the CD-ROMs as they might need to be shared between all of my class
- Information on the CD-ROMs may be out of date
- Any other valid point

4. (a) The concept being assessed is **Power**. Candidates are required to use understanding of the concept to provide detailed descriptions with relevant examples and appropriate generalisations.

"Good points" include:

- The UN took economic sanctions against Serbia in order to change its policy
- Arms sanctions were also taken to try and cut off their supplies of weapons
- Peace-keeping forces sent in to both countries—UN peace keepers are also stationed in Cyprus to keep Greek and Turkish Cypriots apart
- UN peace-keepers also protected aid convoys that were sent in to help the starving and the injured
- UN declared "safe areas"
- UN declared "no fly zones" and bombed targets in Yugoslavia to try and stop Serb advancement
- Any other valid point

(b) The concept being assessed is **Need**. Candidates are required to use understanding of the concept to provide detailed explanations with relevant examples and appropriate generalisations.

"Good points" include:

- A number of countries in Eastern Europe were tied politically and militarily to the former Soviet Union

C 4. (b) **continued**

- The break-up of the Soviet Union meant that these countries got their independence and freedom from Communism
- Joining NATO should ensure no return of Communism
- It draws these countries closer to the West and offers protection should there be an outbreak of trouble either internally or from outwith their borders
- Any other valid point

(c) Candidates are required to provide arguments and evidence to support and oppose a given point of view.

"Good points" include:

For joining the Euro:

Source 1

- EU countries are our biggest trading partners with 70% of our exports going there
- "Prosperity is built on this"—we are doing well economically and we want it to continue
- There is no loss of national identity.

Source 2

- In France the percentage agreeing actually went up to show that support for the Euro remains strong
- This was also the case in Spain—from 72% to 75%, and in Finland from 47% to 49%

Source 3

- There is a feeling that it will prove beneficial in that more jobs will be created—42% as opposed to 36%. This must be good as it will cut unemployment even further
- It will make it easier travelling abroad. There will be no need to keep exchanging different currencies. More than half those interviewed think this to be the case
- It will not cause countries to lose much of their national identity

Against joining the Euro:

Source 2

- The British people just don't want to join. In 1999, 25% only wanted to join and 1 year later this had gone down to 22%
- In Germany and Ireland although a majority are in favour, the Euro is losing support. In Ireland the figure has gone down from 78% to 63%

Source 3

- Europeans believe that by joining the Euro crime levels will increase because of the new notes and coins. Over 60% believe this to be the case
- Bank charges will also rise. Over three-quarters of people think that this will happen

Modern Studies
Credit Level
2002 (cont.)

C 4. (c) continued

- Europeans feel that the introduction of the Euro will not make any difference between the rich and not so rich countries in Europe

Source 4

- The pound is stable unlike the Euro which has lost value from January 1999 to July 2000. It was worth 70p in January 1999 and this had dropped to 62p within 18 months

- Changeover costs will be enormous and this will not be offset by reduced trade costs

- More power being given to Europe and taken away from the UK

There may be other valid points that candidates can identify.

(d) Candidates are required to provide an argument and evidence to support a personal point of view.

For two marks candidates should make a **new** point that they have not included in their answer to (b), or make a very good generalised point based on the Sources.